THE ESSENTIAL
PHONE INTERVIEW HANDBOOK

By
Paul J. Bailo, MBA, MSW

CAREER
PRESS

Pompton Plains, NJ

THE ESSENTIAL PHONE INTERVIEW HANDBOOK
EDITED AND TYPESET BY NICOLE DEFELICE
Cover design by Jeff Piasky
Printed in the U.S.A.

To order this title, please call toll-free 1-800-CAREER-1 (NJ and Canada: 201-848-0310) to order using VISA or MasterCard, or for further information on books from Career Press.

The Career Press, Inc.
220 West Parkway, Unit 12
Pompton Plains, NJ 07444
www.careerpress.com

Library of Congress Cataloging-in-Publication Data
Bailo, Paul J., 1965-
  The essential phone interview handbook / by Paul J. Bailo.
     p. cm.
  Includes bibliographical references and index.
  ISBN 978-1-60163-154-1 -- ISBN 978-1-60163-672-0 (ebook)
    1. Employment interviewing. 2. Telephone in job hunting. I. Title.
  HF5549.5.I6B295 2011
  650.14'4--dc22

                                                        2011003481

PRAISE FOR

The Essential Phone Interview Handbook:

"[Because] busy recruiters use phone interviewing as a preliminary to face-to-face interviews, you'll want to know how to control the conversation once the phone rings and what the proper steps to follow are once the interview dance begins. *The Essential Phone Interview Handbook* sets the right tone and correct habits for successfully presenting your strengths in a succinct and pleasant manner. You will improve your chances of being ready if you read this book before picking up the phone."

—Dr. William D. Reisel, professor of management, St. John's University

"50 percent of getting any job is getting the chance to interview face-to-face. *The Essential Phone Interview Handbook* will immeasurably increase the odds of your getting that opportunity."

—Dave Opton, founder of ExecuNet

"The first critical touch-point of a job seeker's target company contact is the telephone interview. *The Essential Phone Interview Handbook* offers a logical and strategic approach in this challenging job market. This book is a must-read, a fast read, and a wise read for the career candidate looking for every edge!"

—Linda M. Van Valkenburgh, MS, CEO & executive career coach, My Executive Career Coach, LLC

"*The Essential Phone Interview Handbook* should be in every job seeker's tool kit."

—Maria Hanson, LiveCareer

"If you want to do a better job on the phone persuading anyone to do anything, this book is for you. Paul Bailo knows that everything communicates—on the phone and in person."

—George Bradt, president, Prime Genesis and author of *The 100 Day Action Plan*

"*The Essential Phone Interview Handbook* tells us exactly what employers are really thinking. This information helps us recognize what is already inside of us, what is possible if we are prepared and think about what makes good sense. Reading this book will help you meet your potential and put you on the road to success."

—Julie Cardone, vocational rehabilitation counselor, New York State Office of Children & Family Services

DEDICATION

To my wife, Kathy, my son, Connor, my daughter, Kaitlyn, and to my dear friends and family members who made my dream a reality...thank you forever.

In memory of my dad.... Thank you for being my dad. I love you forever.

ACKNOWLEDGMENTS

A special thanks to my family and friends! It is without question that this book would never have happened if it weren't for the constant support of my family and friends.

I want to thank my wife, Kathy, and our wonderful children, Connor and Kaitlyn, who allowed me to miss baseball games, soccer games, and playing video games while Daddy wrote a book to help others.

Thank you to my family and friends who keep me energized, excited, and moving forward.

To Amanda Stoll—one big huge thank-you! Amanda Stoll was diligent in her editing of *The Essential Phone Interview Handbook*. Her meticulous editing skills and her attention to detail just make the book sparkle. Amanda's professional writing experiences and keen wit have added significant value to the book. Thank you, Amanda, for all your efforts.

To the team at Career Press—thank you. Adam Schwartz, acquisitions editor, thank you for bringing life to my book. A special thank-you to editor Nicole DeFelice, whose wisdom and creative editing added significant value to the book. I could not have done it without you.

To Gareth Esersky at the Carol Manning Agency, thank you for taking my call, meeting me at the book store, and making the book deal happen.

Next stop: the book tour!

CONTENTS

INTRODUCTION

Looking for a new job? Your phone interviewing skills could be the deciding factor in getting a live interview!

The Essential Phone Interview Handbook is a must-have. Call it the Holy Grail of any and all phone interview strategy books. If you're currently employed and you're looking for a better life, you'll benefit greatly from reading this book. If you're starting a new job search, *The Essential Phone Interview Handbook* instantly offers you a giant leap forward in your career. With help from this easy-to-understand book, you'll quickly become a phone interview expert.

If you're about to graduate college, *The Essential Phone Interview Handbook* marks another key point in your continuing education. It's a very competitive market out there these days, and you'll want (and need) every bit of sound job-seeking advice.

There is no greater gift for a job-seeker. *The Essential Phone Interview Handbook* allows you to master all aspects of the phone interview; what you learn will go a long way toward getting the position you want and deserve.

HOW DID PHONE INTERVIEW PRO BEGIN?

Phone Interview Pro is an outgrowth of my personal experience. I was once like all of you—participating in many phone interviews in attempts to progress in my career. I noticed that although resume, interview preparation, and target company research assistance are commonly offered by outplacement and career counseling organizations, the importance of the telephone interview is often overlooked.

In response to this, I have created Phone Interview Pro—offering a book, an evaluation, and an online education program to those seeking to hone their phone interview skills. Today, more than ever, job candidates make initial contact with prospective employers via telephone. Why not increase your chances by improving your phone interview performance?

Since its beginning, Phone Interview Pro has grown, becoming an integrated part of many outsourcing agencies and educational institutions. We continue to expand, helping many individuals on their path to phone interview success.

There is no greater gift in the world than to help another human being succeed!

What Is a Phone Interview?

Do not think of a phone interview as a set time and day to talk with a person concerning an opportunity. It is much more than that. Anytime you pick up the phone or receive a call related to your job campaign, it is a phone interview. Everything you do, everything you say—even the way you say it—it impacts the mental image of you created in the mind of the person on the other end of the telephone. The impression you make on the interviewer starts immediately!

A phone interview is not just a one-hour or 30-minute scheduled phone conversation. It is not something that can easily be glossed over on your path to a face-to-face interview. A phone interview is an audition for a serious role in your future career. It is the first door to a successful job campaign.

FIVE KEY ELEMENTS OF A SUCCESSFUL PHONE INTERVIEW

Competition in the job market is extremely fierce and companies want to recruit world-class candidates. These candidates must perform a world-class phone interview. Such a phone interview embraces five key elements.

Be Yourself at Your Best

Don't try to be the person you think the interviewer wants you to be; instead, be the person you actually are. You don't want to get hired, only to find out that the interviewer thought she was hiring someone else. Be yourself. Just make sure to present the best version of yourself.

Prepare, Prepare, Prepare

All great accomplishments have their foundation in carefully thought-out preparation. Phone interviews are a lot like open-book tests—you can have all your information (resumes, cover letters, and so on) right in front of you. Be sure you're organized and that you've taken advantage of practice techniques to ensure success.

Listen. Think. Speak.

Be sure to listen to what the interviewer has to say, and think before responding. Take a few seconds to understand the question, and then prepare a quality answer before simply blurting out something less intelligent.

Be Confident, Professional, and Assertive

Exude confidence! This is your time to impress the interviewer and convince him you are an excellent candidate for the job. Be sure to speak professionally. Also, be assertive! After all, how can you get the job if you don't ask for it?

Be Brief. Be Bold. Be Done.

Stay on point. Answer the interviewer's questions directly and with precision. Make yourself stand out from the rest of the applicant pool by giving impressive responses that display your unique talents. Also, you only get a few moments to tell the interviewer why you deserve this position, so don't drag out the interview. Instead, paint a succinct portrait of yourself that will leave a lasting impression.

A Phone Interview Is Like a Date

An appropriate comparison to make is that the phone interview is like a first date. It is the beginning of a long-term courtship. It is the introduction to a relationship, and, if it goes smoothly, there will be additional connection points to help you along the way to a permanent relationship—in this case, a permanent position at the company at which you are interviewing.

When you go out on a first date, you are getting a feel for the other person. You do not know this person, and you are unsure as to whether you want to begin this relationship. Typically, people will go on many first dates before finding someone they wish to go out with on a regular basis.

It is the same for a phone interview. The interviewer is testing you out to see if you are a good fit for this position. She has many other candidates with whom she is doing the same thing. You need to impress your interviewers by telling them what they want to hear, emphasizing your positive attributes, so they will ask you out on a second date— that is, continue to build this relationship with you through a second phone interview or a face-to-face interview.

Something to Think About...

Think about the first time you met your current boyfriend, girlfriend, spouse, or significant other. Did you say, "Hello, it's nice to meet you. Do you want to marry me?" Of course you didn't. You do not want to start a long-term relationship with someone you do not know.

From the other side of the spectrum, if someone asked you to marry him or her on the first date, would you say yes? Of course you wouldn't. You do not want to make a commitment to someone you just met, and you might also think, "What is wrong with this person that he or she feels the need to propose right away? Isn't there anyone else who would want to be in this relationship? Do I want to be in this relationship?"

Both people in the relationship need time and multiple interactions to get to know one another. The first date is the time to display yourself at your best so the other individual will want to spend more time with you.

A phone interview is a real-life relationship. You need to impress your interviewer and show him you are qualified for this commitment. This will open doors for continuing to build a relationship with this company, thereby increasing your hiring potential.

A phone interview is a first date. It may be stressful and nerve-wracking, but it is also an exciting opportunity to try something new and show off your positive traits. Present the best version of yourself as a starting block on which to build this professional relationship.

The Phone Interview Is a Dance

A phone interview is like a dance. What does this mean? Both people involved in the phone interview must be on the same page, moving at the same speed. Each must bring relevant information and discussion to the table in order for the conversation to flow smoothly. If your minds are not working together, your interaction with your interviewer will not go smoothly.

Think of when you go dancing. If you are doing the jitterbug and your partner is waltzing, what happens? Major collision, toes get stepped on, people fall—not a very impressive performance. The same applies to your phone interview.

You want to balance the interview so that the conversation flows smoothly. If you can interact well with your interviewer, this proves you can work well with others—a strong candidate for a team at a company.

Learn your interviewer's dance moves. Is she hurried and just wants to get a lot of information quickly? Does she want to talk for the majority of the time, or is she interested in hearing your stories from your last employment? Find out the interviewer's style so that you will mesh well during your phone interview.

A connection and understanding between you and your interviewer will create a positive conversation. Don't you want to dance with someone who is good at dancing your favorite style? Please your interviewer with your conversation by thinking of your phone interview as an elegant dance.

TALK RADIO

An excellent strategy for interview preparation involves listening to talk radio. This simple task can hone overall listening skills, and it will also provide an effective way to present yourself using only speech.

The Listener

Talk radio teaches you how to listen effectively and is excellent practice for developing different listening skills, all of which are critical if you want to ace your phone interview. You must be able to pay attention to a speaker who isn't right in front of you. This means being able to maintain focus while avoiding distractions.

Missing one sentence of a talk radio show could disrupt your understanding of the entire presentation. This isn't something you want to have happen during your phone interview.

The Presenter

You can develop your role as the interviewee by noticing the strengths of a talk radio announcer. Similar to radio announcers, you must be able to maintain the attention of your audience during your phone interview. If the interviewer is interested in what you're saying, he'll be interested in you.

Talk radio announcers use different tactics to get their points across, such as descriptive adjectives and varied voice tones. These can be good ways to portray a clear, positive image.

Make sure you are listening to radio news announcements and not radio interviews or two-way talk radio; radio announcers have been trained in conveying information, whereas radio callers have little to no experience expressing themselves on the air.

STORY WITH A MORAL

Growing up, my father was a huge New York Yankees fan and I loved to watch the games with him. When the Yankees game was on television, my father would turn off the sound and tell me to run upstairs and bring down the radio. He would tune to the radio station airing the game and we would follow it this way, with the radio announcer explaining all the action.

Why did my father do this? The radio announcer is portraying the game without a visual to help explain what is happening to his or her audience. For this reason, the person on the radio must clearly and precisely explain the plays that are occurring in the game. Announcers cannot assume the listener sees what they see. They must create a mental theater in the minds of the listeners, conveying the smell of the popcorn and the sound of the screaming fans through just their words. They announce the game with more detail and explanation than television announcers.

In today's day and age, you may not want to give up watching the game on your high-definition flat-screen to listen to the radio, but there are other ways to experience a speaker portraying a scene through only words. When you are driving, turn off the music and turn on talk radio. Notice how as you drive, you are seeing the road, but there is a portion of your mind that is completely in tune with the radio announcer, painting a mental image of what he or she is describing. This is what you need to do for your interviewer during your phone interview.

Moral of the story: Creating a mental theater in your interviewer's mind is not easy. Listen to talk radio to increase your listening skills and learn the difficult art of conveying information in a captivating manner through only your voice.

JOIN TOASTMASTERS INTERNATIONAL

What is Toastmasters International? It is a safe and caring environment in which to learn how to give speeches. Learning to give a speech will help you perform well on a phone interview.

You can prepare for your phone interview by giving a speech at a Toastmasters meeting.

Toastmasters will not only help prepare you for your phone interview, but it will also help you communicate and listen better. It will also improve your presentation skills, increase your self-confidence, and help you become a better leader. Visit *www.toastmasters.org* for more information.

STORY WITH A MORAL

I have been a member of Toastmasters for many years. I once met a person in my Toastmasters group who was very timid. He did not like to stand up and speak in front of a group of people. He spoke very softly and unclearly, with many *ums* and *ahhs*.

In March of 2011, I attended a business conference in New York where there was a guest speaker presenting on how to persuasively market ideas. When this speaker stood to approach the podium in front of hundreds of executives, I recognized him as the same timid man from Toastmasters!

He gave his speech professionally and elegantly, proving to me the power of Toastmasters. He had learned how to project his voice and convey meaning in a well-articulated manner.

Moral of the Story: Joining Toastmasters will significantly increase your ability to showcase yourself and your best attributes during your phone interview. Your speech is all you have in a phone conversation— practice your presentation skills to give a highly professional phone interview. Toastmasters will not only help with your phone interview, but also your overall communication skills.

GET READY

Nothing ever comes easy on the first try. Any athlete's success story will surely involve many hours of practice before making the winning play.

Why should phone interviewing be any different? If you want the job, you must first make a fantastic impression on your interviewer. You cannot expect to throw that game-winning touchdown during your first game. The only way to get to where you want to be in almost any life goal is through practice.

Have you ever heard your own voice on an answering machine or home video? It sounds different from the way you hear yourself when you are talking out loud. Do you cringe or feel embarrassed when you listen to how your voice sounds to others? If so, you're not alone. Many people are surprised when they realize how quickly they talk or how their voice curls up at the end of each statement. The only way to be sure your speech comes out in a professional manner is to practice.

How many times did you record your voicemail message before you were content with the results? I doubt it came out perfect on the first try. Most people record their voicemails multiple times before settling on a message they feel comfortable presenting to the world. Just as you practiced your voicemail, you must also practice your phone interview.

My son Connor loves to play baseball. Connor is a very good second baseman. He has natural skill and knows the game of baseball very well. He watches baseball on TV every morning before school, always looking for new ways to improve his game. He is constantly asking to go to the batting cages to practice his swing. We are at the local baseball field practicing fielding every weekend, always working to improve.

The more you practice, the better you will become. Just as my 10-year-old son improves his baseball skills, you can improve your phone interview skills, through practice. You may consider purchasing a small tape recorder so you can tape yourself and evaluate your voice. However, sometimes it is difficult to judge yourself, especially if you're not exactly sure what you are looking for.

Phone Interview Pro

You can sign up at *www.phoneinterviewpro.com* for a complete phone interview evaluation and let the professionals tell you what they think. Behind each of those sports players' success stories are not only hours of practice, but also a fabulous coach. Let Phone Interview Pro be part of your professional coaching team. We can win the championship together!

1

CONTROL YOUR SURROUNDINGS

Don't let your environment force you into an unprofessional situation by having noise in the background or the TV blasting during your phone interview. These situations are all preventable if you take a moment to alter and fine-tune your environment to help—not hinder—your phone interview success.

HOME-FIELD ADVANTAGE

The increased use of phone interviews in today's job search is very much to your advantage because you get to control the setting.

There's no traffic to cause delays, no unfamiliar rooms to cause confusion, and no chief executive staring at you from across the desk. With phone interviews, you can create a comfort zone—your comfort zone. Feeling confident and self-assured in a phone interview will dramatically increase your assertiveness.

Something to Think About…

Why do baseball teams often perform better at home games than away? They have the home-field advantage. They have all their fans cheering for them. They are familiar with the field, knowing where all the dead spots in the ground are located. They recognize familiar sights, such as that billboard on the back wall where they aim their home run hits during practice. The passion and energy is in the air as their home announcer calls out the lineup. The crowds, the sights, the field, and the sounds all benefit a baseball team in their home-field advantage. Your phone interview is the same. When you answer that phone you need to be just as comfortable as the Red Sox when they walk into Fenway Park.

Make use of your home-field advantage—prepare and conduct your phone interview in the setting and manner that works best for you. Use it to hit that phone interview right out of the park!

Remember the four "bests" to ensure you take full advantage of this opportunity.

Best Day

Don't sign up for your phone interview on the day you promised to watch your neighbor's dogs, the day of your daughter's seventh birthday party, or your sister's annual family visit. Thinking about other events will distract you, and this could produce less-than-intelligent responses. Make sure that you pick a day when you can devote your full attention to the interview.

Best Time

Don't sign up for your phone interview at times when you're normally sleeping, eating, or running errands. Some people are most focused during the morning hours; others need more time to wake up and are more motivated in the evening. Pick a time when you know you'll do your best work.

Best Room

Don't conduct your phone interview lying down in your bed or in the living room with the TV on. Rooms that are too comfortable may contain too many distractions, causing you to lose focus on the phone interview. Pick a room that makes you feel professional and allows you to concentrate. This will help you produce quality responses.

Best Phone

Don't conduct your phone interview on a telephone that could cause the interview to be interrupted (like when a cell phone hits a "no service" area or runs low on battery power). That's why it makes the most sense to use a landline instead of a cell or wireless phone. Also, don't use a speakerphone. They may carry static, increase background noises, and your voice may cut in and out. Make sure you pick a high-quality telephone so you can clearly communicate with the interviewer.

READY YOUR SPACE

Before you begin your phone interview, get yourself set up and organized. You don't want to be scrambling for papers or pausing during your interview. If your workspace looks professional, you'll feel and act more professional.

- ✆ Have the company research, your resume, and your written-out questions handy.

- ✆ Remove anything that makes noise or could cause your mind to wander during your interview.

- ✆ Turn off your fax machine. Beeping noises are distracting, and you can't answer questions intelligently while you're reading a fax.

- ✆ Turn off your cell phone. You can't answer another call while participating in a phone interview, so why even have another phone nearby?

The ringing will divert your attention, and receiving text messages will make you want to stop and read them.

ℂ Turn off your computer. Fish floating across your screensaver, for example, may lead to daydreaming about the ocean and summer vacation, causing you to miss pivotal interview questions.

ℂ Put away your grocery list, that pile of pictures your sister sent you, and sticky notes about your latest in-home project. If personal things are scattered about, it makes it that much more difficult to concentrate.

ℂ Be sure to have a pen and paper handy so you can take notes throughout your interview. Having your materials organized will allow you to reference information with ease.

Removing all unnecessary objects and distractions allows you to completely focus on the task at hand—acing your phone interview.

STORY WITH A MORAL

Some years back, I worked for three months to obtain an interview for a top position at Alley Bank. I sent my resume, I did my research, and I was primed and ready to go. I had spent weeks preparing for this phone interview.

Little did I know, my wife had used the fax machine in my office that morning, which is attached to the main phone line. When she was finished, she had neglected to disconnect the fax machine.

"Hello?" *DOOOT DOOOT DOOOT, RRRURRIP, BANG!*

The first thing I (and the interviewer) heard was the fax machine going off. I frantically grabbed the paper, knocking the machine on the ground with a loud *BANG!* Three long months of preparation for my phone interview, and it began with a loud commotion.

Moral of the Story: Let's make sure this does not happen to you. Survey the area and check your phone before the start of your phone interview.

REMOVE ALL BACKGROUND NOISE

Background noise can be heard by the interviewer and thus distract her from your responses. It can also hinder her ability to hear what you're saying, and that can create confusion and miscommunication.

Background noise also distracts you from what the interviewer is saying. Asking her to repeat questions or comments is unprofessional and takes away from time you should be using to gain as much information as possible while you present a clear image of yourself.

These extra sounds can also start your mind to wander to whatever is creating the noise, causing you to lose focus.

Conduct your phone interview in a room *without* any of the following:

- ☎ Television. Even if it's playing behind you and you're not watching it, it's still a major distraction, especially when you consider that volume and special sound effects often change.

- ☎ Pets. Your dog can definitely bark much louder than anything you're saying. So consider placing your pets on a different floor in the house (or make sure they're elsewhere) during your phone interview.

- ☎ Children. Children can be loud and unpredictable. They can be doing a puzzle silently one minute and be screaming at the top of their lungs the next. If you must conduct your phone interview while the kids are in the house, at least close your office door for some privacy.

- ☎ Doorbells. A ringing doorbell in the background is distracting and unprofessional. Post a "Do Not Disturb" sign over the doorbell. This will eliminate the unnecessary distraction of an unexpected doorbell ringing during your interview.

These are just a few examples of common noisemakers in a house. Make sure to survey your workspace during preparation and question if anything could make noise. Turn these items off or move them to a different room.

Background noise is distracting to both parties in a phone interview; it frustrates the interviewer and casts you in an unprofessional light. In turn, this leads you to become stressed as you try to remove the noise. Don't let a distraction like background noise lead to a less-than-quality performance on your phone interview.

Something to Think About...

What do you think and feel when you are at work on a conference call and you hear a baby crying or Sponge-Bob SquarePants blasting in the background of your top team member's phone line? This person has a reputation of being a hardworking, very intelligent individual; however, at this moment, these qualities are not being portrayed. Rather, you may be thinking, "What is this person really doing while working from home?" This does not make a very good impression for this top team member.

This example involves an individual who has already earned his position at the top, already proven his responsible, goal-driven abilities, and still you find yourself questioning his skills. Can you imagine if this background noise was occurring before he earned the top role on the team, before he had earned any role on the team at all? Surely he would not be thought of as a hardworking, business-oriented individual who would bring positive improvements to the company.

Do not let background noise stop you from proving your positive, professional qualities during your phone interview. A silent background conveys seriousness and a focus on the task at hand—acing your phone interview.

THEY MAY NOT BE ABLE TO SEE YOU, BUT THEY CAN HEAR YOU

Even though your interviewer cannot see you, she can hear if you are trying to multitask or scrambling to find information. Why chance it? Stay focused on the phone interview and only on the phone interview—nothing else. Even things you may think are inconspicuous can still make noise, such as:

- Typing on a keyboard.
- Opening a file cabinet.
- Tapping a pen.
- Opening a door.

If you want to land this job, you need to ace the phone interview. If you want to ace the phone interview, remember, the interviewer can hear everything you're doing. Don't conduct any actions that are distracting and unprofessional; give 110 percent of your attention to your phone interview.

STORY WITH A MORAL

I was conducting a phone interview with someone for a top executive position at my previous company. The interview was going very well, but all the while there was a strange tapping sound on the phone line.

Throughout the course of the interview, I continually tried to identify the sound, which distracted me from the content of the interviewee's speech. She did not make a great impression on me because she could not keep my attention over this clicking noise.

After the conclusion of the phone interview, I had my wife call me and test out different office sounds to try to discover what had been creating the noise. We tried tapping pens and clicking the keyboard, but nothing sounded the same. We finally realized the interviewee had been tapping her fingernails against the handset of the telephone. This is a sound that seemed almost silent to the person holding the phone, but created a magnified echo on the other end of the line. Although I could not see the interviewee, I could hear her tapping, and this distracted from her phone interview.

Moral of the Story: Your phone interviewer cannot see you, but he can hear you. When one of your senses is limited (in this case sight), your other senses are stronger. Your phone interviewer can hear even small sounds that you may think are too quiet to carry over phone lines. These quiet background noises are enough to significantly diminish the quality of your phone interview. Don't make noise—make progress!

WHAT TO DO IF THERE IS NOISE
IN THE BACKGROUND

Before you began your phone interview, you carefully prepared the room so there would be no background noise or distractions. Yet somehow an unexpected sound was still heard. Now what do you do?

Acknowledge it and move on from it very quickly. Apologize briefly for the interruption (showing that you're aware that background noises shouldn't be a part of your phone interview), and then continue your interview. Don't let interruptions take away from your content. Often, you can spin this disruption to demonstrate more of your own positive attributes and ability to think on your feet.

For example, if there is a dog barking in the background, and it's very loud, acknowledge it by saying, "It seems that my neighbor's dog is out and about. He must be barking because he's excited about the spring weather we're having. My apologies for the distraction, but as I was saying, I'm very excited about the position, and hope we can continue with the phone interview."

Another approach to this situation might be, "I'm sorry. I thought I had planned for everything—researching, practicing, and studying. One thing I didn't plan on was my neighbor's dog. Lucky for me, though, I'm very flexible, and I can easily manage the unexpected. Let's continue with our phone interview."

You're only human, and people encounter unexpected situations every day—especially on the job. Your ability to handle these interruptions proves your ability to be flexible and adaptable.

Let's look at another example: Suppose there's a crying baby in the background. You might say something like, "It seems my baby woke up a bit early today. Do you have any children? My son is three months old and is just getting used to sleeping in a crib. Guess he hasn't adapted very well—unlike his dad. One of my key attributes is adaptability."

Turn the interruption into something the interviewer can relate to; this way she understands and you won't be penalized for unfortunate timing. If at any point you think the noise won't go away, though, you may want to consider stopping the phone interview. You can reschedule or go elsewhere (away from the distraction) and simply call back a few minutes later.

Sometimes things happen that are just out of your control. Remember this famous phrase: When life gives you lemons, make lemonade. Be professional, courteous, and make your points quickly and effectively. Remember also to acknowledge and remove all distractions immediately.

Story With a Moral

I was once working as a team leader and was on an important business call with one of my team members when there was a loud commotion in the background. My employee continued speaking, and I was annoyed that he had not properly prepared for this phone conversation. It seemed to me there were background distractions, proving this individual was not serious about the task at hand.

Then, after he finished his statement, he took a pause and then apologized for the noise. It seems a person wheeling binders past his office on the way to storage had knocked the top row off the cart as he was passing by.

His acknowledgement of the disruption in an apologetic manner told me this person knew how to handle interruptions in a professional manner. He immediately picked up where we had left off, and the background noise had no lasting damage on the discussion.

Moral of the Story: We are only human. Sometimes things happen beyond our control. Handle background noise with professionalism and an understanding that these sounds should not be heard on a phone interview. Don't let sound bring you down.

2

TOOLS FOR SUCCESS

Carpenters, plumbers, and masons are all masters of their professions and have their cherished tools of the trade. They care for their prized equipment by keeping blades sharpened and power tools cleaned and oiled. Their array of professional equipment is always in fine working condition. The same must be said for the tools you need to perform your professional phone interview.

USE A LANDLINE

The best sound quality telephone for your phone interview is a landline. Remember not to use your cell phone or portable phone—or any device that doesn't need to be plugged into a telephone jack.

Just think of the potential problems:

✆ "What did you say? Wait, what did you say?"
✆ "Can you hear me now? Can you hear me now?"
✆ "Hold on, I think I'm losing you."

Those are all phrases you don't want to say during your phone interview. It's very unprofessional and causes interruptions that will undoubtedly hinder your overall performance.

Also, make sure there isn't another phone extension connected to the landline during your interview. It would be very unprofessional (and embarrassing) if someone picked up that other line during your interview. If you're making your call from home, make sure others in your household know not to pick up the phone.

Such interruptions could cause confusion and distractions that significantly lower the quality of your phone interview. In addition, if you're using a DSL line, make sure you have your filters on so you don't have any static on the phone line. Use a landline with only one connected telephone. This will ensure that you'll speak clearly.

When preparing for your phone interview, call a friend to confirm that all is working properly on your phone line.

Why take an unnecessary chance when you can prevent it? Making a test call will ease your mind, and it will ensure that your phone is working properly. Bottom line: don't use your cell phone for your phone interview!

Story With a Moral

I was leading a team of employees on a very important project at my last company. One day, I had a scheduled phone meeting with one of our team members who was at a different location.

I called this individual, and we began our discussion on the recent updates of the project. There was some static on the phone line, making it somewhat difficult to hear, which was hindering our conversation. Then, all of a sudden, I heard a voice say, "At the next intersection, make a left."

The GPS was talking in the background of our phone meeting! This person, an important businessman on our team, was conducting a meeting from his car, on his cell phone. You can imagine how this affected my opinion of him. He seemed unprofessional and unfocused, proving to me this project was not important to him.

Moral of the Story: Conduct your phone interview from a working landline. This will eliminate all problems and it will convey the professional, business-oriented person that you are. Use a landline—land that job!

The Bat Phone

Not only should your phone interview be conducted from a landline, it is also a wise idea to get a separate phone and phone line designated specifically to your job search, so you are never caught off guard.

Think of your career campaign. You send out your resume to many job opportunities every day. Any of those employers can call you weeks, even months later. Without the Bat Phone, these calls will go to your household landline. You pick up the telephone, thinking it is going to be one of your kids calling from a friend's house, and all of a sudden you're thrown into an unexpected career call.

Get another phone with its own line, and when that phone rings, you will know it has to do with a job opportunity. Have that phone in your office (or wherever it is you conduct business) and have your resume readily available so you never have to search through piles of paper. This way, you can avoid all sneak-attack phone calls.

Something to Think About…

Think of Batman (the inspiration for this career campaign phone line). When Batman is working on the Batmobile and he hears the Bat Phone ring, he knows it's Commissioner Gordon calling Batman on an important mission. Before Batman even picks up the phone, his head is in the game. He knows this is a serious phone call. Your Bat Phone plays the same role for you and your job search.

When you hear that phone ring, you should immediately get into the mindset of a professional, business-oriented person. You're serious, you're confident, and you're assertive. You are ready to be your best on this phone call.

Have a Bat Phone for your career search. Be ready for *the* call.

DISABLE CALL WAITING

If you have call waiting on your telephone, be sure to turn it off. If you don't know how, you should be able to find it in your phone manual, or you can call your phone company and ask for the code that will disable the call waiting service.

Call waiting can have a drastically damaging effect on your phone interview. It can create a chain reaction that will cause the following to happen:

- ✆ You become distracted by the call-waiting beep.
- ✆ You have to ask the interviewer to repeat the question to avoid giving a low-quality answer.
- ✆ The interviewer recognizes you aren't giving your full attention to this interview and thus thinks you're not serious about the potential opportunity.

Suddenly, a call from your Aunt Sally—wondering if you've used the rice pudding recipe she suggested—results in a poor overall performance on your phone interview. Call waiting is very rude and unprofessional during a phone interview or any type of important phone call. Before you do anything else, be sure to turn off call waiting during your preparation.

HEADSET VS. HANDSET

"Can I use a headset for a phone interview?" This question has come up many times during my extensive travels to present to executive groups. My answer is, simple is best. Low risk equals high return. The logic is straightforward; an old-fashioned, hand-held telephone with a cord is the best telephone for your phone interview. Anything else adds the possibility for problems.

Some people may argue that a headset allows for your hands to be free, making it easier to take notes, look through documents, and so on. However, a headset compounds greater probability of something going wrong. The wiring, the microphone—there are too many pieces. The more components, the greater the risk of disaster. However, if you feel more comfortable with a headset for your phone interview, by all means, use it, but my recommendation is a simple, classic telephone. A low-risk, hand-held phone eliminates the possibility of unnecessary problems.

Story With a Moral

I once had a coworker who was in the process of searching for a new career. He kept me informed on his latest interviews, explaining the high points and asking my advice on the low points. One time, he told me of a terrible phone interview experience he had while using a headset.

He was on a call with the chief marketing officer of an important financial corporation and the conversation was going great. The interviewer asked him a question in reference to his previous company and my friend stood up to reach for a document about a certain project he had led.

As he stood up, he forgot his headset was connected; he pulled out the wiring and disconnected the phone call. All of his work, his great, professional conversation, and the phone interview ended with a malfunction of the telephone. My friend immediately called the interviewer back, but the damage was done, with the interview abruptly interrupted by the disconnection of his headset. Unfortunately, my friend did not obtain this position.

Moral of the Story: Keep it simple. Stick with what has proven through decades of history to be a solid form of communication. The hand-held telephone is the least complicated phone—the least likely to cause any problems.

CALLER ID

When you are preparing to take on the first step of your job campaign—the phone interviews—be sure to set up caller ID. You need to have caller ID on your Bat Phone so that you are always in the know.

Caller ID notifies you as to who is calling prior to picking up the receiver. It allows you those few key seconds to register in your mind who this person is and why he or she is calling you. Now you are prepared and in control before answering the telephone.

If you do not recognize the name, do not pick up the call. Only answer calls during your phone campaign that you recognize. This puts you in a position of power to respond professionally and accurately to the person on the other end of the phone.

If you do not know the number, let the call go to voicemail. The person will leave his name and reason for calling, thus placing you in control. Now you know who he is and what organization he is calling from. You can call back with confidence and the ability to speak intelligently about this particular opportunity.

STORY WITH A MORAL

My friend Anthony once told me a story of what happened to him when he did not have caller ID. Anthony had sent out his resume a few months prior to multiple companies. He had heard back from two and had scheduled interviews for these positions.

One day, his job campaign telephone rang and he answered, not knowing who was on the other end of the phone. It turned out to be a recruiter from one of the companies Anthony had researched several months prior. Suddenly, Anthony was ambushed. He was not prepared for a phone call regarding this organization. He stumbled over his words, sounding unprepared and unprofessional.

Moral of the Story: Do not let this happen to you. You want to use every chance you get to present the best version of yourself to a potential employer. If the person calls, but you are not ready, you have lost this opportunity. Be sure your phone interview telephone has caller ID. This way, you are always in control, always prepared, and always ready to ace your phone interview.

3

WARM-UP

Relax, feel good, and approach your phone interview with confidence, professionalism, and less stress. Prepare mentally, physically, and emotionally to perform exceptionally well during your phone interviews. Preparation is key to your phone interviewing success.

RESEARCH THE COMPANY

It takes three days to fully prepare your research for your phone interview. Not three hours—three days. It is very important to fully know and understand all the information you gain regarding your phone interview. If you research and study hard, you will be able to speak intelligently without stress.

Day One

The first day of your research is library day. Go to your local library and look up information on the company for which you are interviewing. Where did it begin? How has it grown? What are its marketing strategies? Look up S&P reports as well as annual reports on the company.

While you are at the library, find a really interesting article about the company in a highly acclaimed newspaper—the *New York Times*, *Wall Street Journal*, and so on. Put this article in your back pocket. You are going to use it later during your phone interview follow-up.

Day Two

On the second day of your phone interview research, take all the information you gathered on day one, and turn it into facts you can use during your interview. Organize it in a way that makes sense to you. You do not need to memorize it, but you do need to have a strong understanding so you can speak intelligently and prove you have put time and effort into this company.

This is also the day when you want to create your knockout questions. These are questions that contain financial, economic, and political information. Write them down so you do not have to remember them. Create knockout questions, incorporating your research, to really impress your interviewer. Some examples include:

℗ [Interviewer's name], during your first 30 days in the company, what surprised you the most about [name of company]? What thrilled you the most about it? What humbled you the most?

℗ [Interviewer's name], what are you most proud of about [name of company]? What corporate issues cause you to lose sleep at night?

Day Three

By the third day, you should be finished finding and studying your research. On this last day, you want to get everything ready. Organize your space so your research and your questions are easily visible. Go over important facts that you know you want to mention in your phone interview. You've done the work, so be sure to organize it so you can showcase your knowledge.

Remember, research is something that takes time and effort. You cannot just go to Google, type in the company name, and assume that is enough information to get you through the phone interview. You need to really invest your time and energy into this company and the position for which you are interviewing. Having sufficient background knowledge will positively impact your phone conversation and your success on your phone interview.

STORY WITH A MORAL

When I was in school, I had to write a ton of research papers. I remember one time when I just did not have enough time to really do an A+ job. I printed various sources and cited them all, but I only used one for my actual paper.

Well, when I went to my class, my professor was impressed with what I had written. He started a conversation, asking me to explain different points I had touched on in my paper. Unfortunately, I had not done the research, and I could not speak intelligently about my topic. I tried to discuss the information, circumventing what I did not know, but it was obvious I was not prepared. This was not only embarrassing, but it also did not make me look like an intelligent student in front of my professor.

Moral of the Story: Take the time to do your research. This is a valuable aspect of your phone interview that must not be taken lightly. Your research will demonstrate your intelligence, your driven attitude, and your professional manner. If you only do half of the research, you will only know half of the information you need to be successful. This will create major roadblocks in your attempts to impress your interviewer with your knowledge about the company. Three days of research equals one impressive phone interview.

RESEARCH YOUR INTERVIEWER

The more you know, the better you will be. Not only do you need to research the company for which you are interviewing—its products, finances, current news—you also need to research the person.

You want to find out what drives this person—her likes and dislikes. A great way to do this is to look her up on LinkedIn. Maybe her profile photograph is one of her and her dog. I don't care if you are allergic or once got attacked—for this phone interview, you like dogs. Maybe it lists the university this person attended and you have a coworker who went to the same school. So you could mention, "I see on your LinkedIn profile that you went to _____ University. A coworker of mine did also and was extremely impressed with the students and faculty. We worked on a team together developing a financial system for my last company."

This way, you connect with your interviewer, talk about something she is interested in, and also display one of your many accomplishments.

Be careful with your research on your interviewer. Do not cross the line between looking up her professional involvement in the company and calling for her high school transcripts. Do not get to the point where your research turns creepy. For example, do not Google search this individual to discover she loves her mom's lasagna and then decide to open with a joke about pasta. There is a difference between bonding over a common interest in something and privacy invasion.

The goal of this research is to be able to find a connection with your interviewer that will allow you to add a personal touch to your professional conversation. Similarities create an instant bond. This allows for a greater and more productive experience.

Something to Think About...

Think of a time you may have attended a large conference or event. Typically, people enter these situations with their guard up. These are strangers; you do not want to reveal anything personal about yourself to them. This makes it difficult to create a connection with anyone.

Then, out of the corner of your eye, you spot him, a man in the back holding a bicycle helmet. Well, you love mountain biking and are even considering signing up for a triathlon. You instantly have a conversation starter that will allow you to connect with this individual. This similarity allows you two to become friendly acquaintances.

This is what you want to make happen during your phone interview. Find something the interviewer likes to do or talk about and then work this into your conversation.

It will allow you to connect as a person rather than simply another potential job candidate.

Research your interviewer, in a very professional manner, to find and/or create common fields of interest, allowing an instant bond to be formed, and increasing the positive results of your phone interview.

What Time Is It?

Remember, the beauty of a phone interview is that it can be conducted at any time from anywhere in the world. You don't need to invest in an expensive trip across the country to participate in an interview.

However, with this convenience comes additional responsibility. You need to be aware of the fact that your interviewer may not be in your time zone. When scheduling your phone interview, be considerate of his clock.

Make sure you do your research to find a time that will be convenient for both of you. If you think your phone interview is being conducted at 1 p.m. your time, it might be 5 a.m. for your interviewer. You want to be aware of the time difference and acknowledge this fact. It shows you're both concerned for the other person, and that you're diligent in your research. If it's 8 p.m. where your interviewer is, don't say, "I hope you enjoy the rest of your day." For him, the day is over, and you won't appear professional if you don't know that.

You also want to be aware of the other person's time zone in order to predict his state of mind. If it's really early or really late in his time zone, he may not be working at peak performance, and therefore will be less enthusiastic about your interview.

Do your research and pick a time when you can both benefit from your phone interview. To find times throughout the world, you can search the Internet for world clock or world time zones. This is a quick and easy way to prove you're knowledgeable and serious about your phone interview.

STORY WITH A MORAL

How would you feel if a person said "Good morning!" to you and it was 4 p.m.? Chances are, you would feel that she did not value this as an important conversation. What if someone says to you, "Wow, the rain is really coming down out there!" but it is sunny where you are? This does not make the person with whom you are speaking seem very intelligent.

I once made the mistake of ending a phone conversation with "Have a great day!" when it was midnight in India. What I should have said was, "Thank you for staying up late to take this call." This sensitive comment would have left a positive image of me in the other person's mind.

Moral of the Story: Be conscious of time zones and use appropriate greetings.

~~~~~~

READ THE NEWSPAPER

The morning of your phone interview, you want to read the newspaper in order to be up to date on current events. The world is drastically changing every second—yesterday's news is old news, and may not even be correct anymore.

Be sure you are reading or watching top-notch world news sources, such as the *Wall Street Journal*, the *New York Times*, and CNN to provide valid, important news stories. The interviewer does not care if your local high school football team lost the third game of the season. Don't read the local section of the newspaper—read the national and international news.

Reading the news will add value to your phone interview because you will be able to speak intelligently about current events. This proves you have not only done your research on the company for which you are interviewing, but you are also an intelligent person who is active in today's changing world. You understand and form opinions on news topics, demonstrating you are intellectually curious and socially oriented.

This will impress your phone interviewer and add to the conversation during your interview. If you can follow and understand what is happening in the news, you will have ideas of how this company functions within these national events. Reading the news will demonstrate your connection to the world around you, proving to the interviewer that you have the capability to also connect to this company's overall goals.

STORY WITH A MORAL

I had an important phone meeting scheduled for 10 a.m. I was very busy that day and did not have time to read the newspaper in the morning.

At the beginning of the conversation, the person with whom I was speaking asked if I had seen the article about the European reaction to the president's speech that was given the night before. Unfortunately, I had to respond that I had not had a chance to look at the news yet that day. This led to an awkward moment when he told me it was an interesting article that I really should read, and completely destroyed the casual first few minutes that typically exist on the phone (the phone interview handshake, detailed in Chapter 5). I felt embarrassed and disconnected from the world around me during this uncomfortable phone introduction.

Moral of the Story: Take the time to read the national and international news the morning of your phone interview. The ability to intelligently discuss world events will positively impact your phone interview. Read the news to prove you're in the know!

OPEN-BOOK TEST

A phone interview is like taking an open-book test—
you don't need to memorize facts and details or stay up
until 2 a.m. making flash cards.

However, you do need to be organized. If your professor told you your next exam was going to be open-book,
you wouldn't show up with just a pencil. Instead, you'd try
to take advantage of the ability to have everything out in
front of you:

- ☎ Your resume. It's much easier to recall and relate to your past achievements when you have a
  list of them right in front of you.

- ☎ Any letters of correspondence. It's a good idea
  to reference any materials you have from the
  company with which you are interviewing.

- ☎ Information about the company/position, such
  as pamphlets and Website printouts. These
  could be useful in referencing specific job responsibilities, as well as the overall workings of
  the company.

- ☎ Questions. Write out a list of questions you
  want to ask the interviewer before your phone
  interview. It will be much easier to present
  your questions in a professional manner when
  they're on paper.

✆ A pen and paper. You'll want to take notes throughout the interview. Scrambling to find writing materials once the phone interview has begun is distracting and sounds unprofessional to the interviewer.

Lay out all your information on your desk before the interview begins. This way, you can reference all your documents easily in a calm, collected, and professional manner. Remember: Organization is the key to success.

Something to Think About...

I am a business professor at a local university. On the rare occasion that I give my students an open-book test, how do you think they perform? As long as they are prepared with their book tabbed and highlighted, everyone earns an A, because it's all right in front of them. Students who do not earn an A on an open-book test fail to take advantage of the opportunity presented to them. They were unprepared, had not read the text, and did not know how to use their materials to the best of their advantage.

A phone interview is the same as an open-book test. You can have all your materials, all your answers laid out right in front of you. As long as you are not rustling papers, your interviewer will never know you have written out all your outstanding qualities and your world-class questions, or that you have them neatly organized in front of you.

Be prepared! Set up your command station with all your information neatly laid out. Why panic over memorizing your company research when you can read it from a piece of paper? Take advantage of the open-book test—ace your phone interview.

CALL THE DAY BEFORE

Twenty-four hours before your phone interview, call your interviewer to confirm the time of your interview. You also want to ask where the focus of the interview will be. Here is an example:

"Hello Mr. Jones, my name is _____. I wanted to confirm our scheduled phone interview for tomorrow at 2 p.m. My phone number is _____. Mr. Jones, I know you're very busy, and I was wondering what you would like to focus on during this interview?"

With any luck, Mr. Jones will confirm the time and tell you, "Yes, I would like to focus on your past employment."

What has the interviewer now done for you? He has just handed you the phone interview! Now you know exactly what to prepare. You will be ready for this phone conversation. It is amazing the answers you get when you ask.

This also provides you the opportunity to hear the interviewer's voice prior to your phone interview. This will help calm your nerves and also connect you with the interviewer on a more human level.

You may get a receptionist or administrative assistant when you call the day before your phone interview. Tell her you are calling to confirm your phone interview and leave your phone number. Say it twice to be sure she has it correct. Then, ask what Mr. Jones likes. Is he a Yankees fan? Does he have a favorite pastime? This will allow you to know how you can connect with your interviewer during your phone interview handshake the following day.

In addition, if you do not have your interviewer's e-mail address, now is the time to get it. Write it down so you can send a thank-you e-mail after you conclude the phone interview. You do not want to ask for his e-mail address during the phone interview.

Calling the day before your phone interview allows you to connect with your interviewer, collect information, and ready yourself for your phone interview. Call ahead—get ahead in your career.

GROUP PHONE INTERVIEWS

Group phone interviews are extremely difficult due to the fact that there are multiple people, personalities, and agendas all on the same phone call. However, by using the correct phone interviewing skills, you can confront this and be successful.

1. Prior to your group phone interview, obtain a list of people who are going to be present. Get their names, titles, and positions.

2. At the start of the group phone interview, try to identify an ally in the group, someone who will assist you in identifying who is talking and what division the speaker is from.

3. Ask everyone to say his or her name and division before speaking during the phone conversation. For example, "Amanda Stoll, senior vice president of communications."

   This will allow you to think and respond appropriately based on the person's title and position. Addressing each individual correctly will earn you points during your group phone interview.

When there is a misunderstanding on this multi-person call, the goal is for your allied coordinator to assist you and mediate any issues. By having someone on your side, you dramatically decrease communication problems, thus increasing your probability of landing a face-to-face interview.

STORY WITH A MORAL

I once had a group phone interview with seven people, all of whom spoke English as a second language. These individuals spoke Korean, but limited English. This was a very important interview for the position of senior vice president of finance.

I had done all my research and was well-prepared. What I was not prepared for was the additional factors that come into play in a group phone interview. The problem I encountered was that I could only understand every other word due to the other individuals' heavy accents. This led to much confusion and frustration. I did not respond well and I did not get the job.

Moral of the Story: Group phone interviews can be intimidating, but they don't have to be. Know the additional problems you may encounter and eliminate them before your phone interview begins. This way you can focus on the task at hand—succeeding on the phone interview and getting to the next step. Master the necessary tactics of a group phone conversation and impress all the participants on the call. Find an ally—impress the whole group!

4

READY YOURSELF

Preparation is the key to your phone interview performance. The more you prepare, the greater your chance of getting the face-to-face interview. It will help reduce your stress level, make you feel more confident, and most importantly, help you relax and be at peak performance for your phone interview. Preparation will help you reduce errors and missteps during the phone interview, from not answering questions clearly and correctly to having a low energy level.

GIVE YOURSELF PLENTY OF TIME

Overall, give yourself plenty of time to prepare for your phone interview, as well as to conduct the actual interview. You don't want to rush and only prepare a few minutes before the phone rings. There is too much at stake to just wing it when it comes to your phone interview.

Your phone interview really starts days before the actual interview. You need time to mentally prepare yourself and your workspace long before show time. Make sure you leave plenty of time to complete the following agenda:

- One to two days before the phone interview:
  - Mentally prepare.
  - Get energized.
  - Get in the phone-interviewing zone. Emotionally, physically, and mentally prepare for the interview.
  - Get the phone interview room ready.
  - Confirm the date and time of your phone interview.
- One hour before the phone interview:
  - Have cough drops standing by.
  - Have water available.

- ✆ Make sure you have paper and pen.

- ✆ Confirm that the phone line is working properly.

- ✆ Make your workspace distraction-proof.

- ✆ Have your resume out so you can easily refer to it. Be sure it is the resume you submitted to this company, not a different version.

- ✆ Write down questions you want to ask before the phone interview begins.

- ✆ Have a photo of a person in a leadership role available to look at during your phone interview.

It is going to take a good deal of time to successfully prepare for your phone interview—*don't* wait until the last minute!

STORY WITH A MORAL

Everyone has super busy days—afternoons when one red traffic light could throw off your entire game plan. These are not the days on which you want to schedule your phone interview.

I can remember a time when I had an important phone interview scheduled for the afternoon, only half an hour after an important meeting. I should have left more time, but it was late in the day and I wanted to be sure I had plenty of time for the phone interview. I got all set up in the morning so that I could race back to my office and take the call.

You can imagine what happened—I may have had all my documents neatly organized, but I was not physically or mentally prepared to begin my phone interview. My mind was still racing from my previous activity and I had not had time to take a breath. My phone interview began with a bumpy start as I tried to calm down and focus while my interview had already begun. By not being fully prepared and at my best, I was putting myself in jeopardy of not making it to the face-to-face interview.

Moral of the Story: Do not try to squeeze your phone interview into a small available window in your day. This is not just a phone call—it is an essential step in your career process. You need to be fully concentrated and prepared in all aspects for your phone interview.

BE WELL-RESTED

There is nothing better than a good night's sleep. You wake up feeling fresh, relaxed, and full of life and energy. With a good night's sleep, you can conquer any task you are facing that day.

The night before your phone interview, go to bed early. A few hours of extra sleep can make all the difference between being mentally sharp and yawning every few minutes during your phone interview.

When you are well-rested, you feel great. And when you feel great, you do great! Wake up with energy and your head in the game. If you are feeling groggy, your mind will not be working at top speed for this important interview.

STORY WITH A MORAL

I was once interviewing a person for a vice president of technology opportunity, and every few minutes, I heard a yawn on the phone. For the first one, I gave the person the benefit of the doubt, but after the 10th or 11th yawn, it was clear this candidate was not prepared for this phone interview.

This has detrimental effects on a candidate's hiring potential. If you cannot be alert and focused for a phone interview, how can you be trusted to act with high productivity on the job?

Moral of the Story: Be well-rested on your phone interview to show you are an energized, productive worker. If you are well-rested, you will make fewer mistakes and show yourself to be the professional, intelligent candidate that you are. Rest and be your best.

EAT SOMETHING

Your body needs sustenance in order to perform well. Athletes, for example, eat pasta the night before a big game so they have enough carbohydrates to power them through the event.

Swimmers drink gallons of water to ensure they will not become dehydrated during a meet. In this same way, you must physically prepare your body for your phone interview.

Make sure you have a good, healthy meal before your phone interview. This is necessary in order for you to be ready and alert for your phone interview. If your phone interview is late in the afternoon, you may need a healthy snack to keep your stomach from rumbling while you're on the phone. Although your interviewer may not be able to hear this, you can. That might lead you to think about your most recent meal, possibly distracting you from your phone interview. Conversely, you don't want to eat too much; that may make you sleepy. Eat just the right amount so that you're energized for your interview.

Bottom line—make sure you eat healthy. Your body needs the necessary nutrition that will have you at peak performance for your phone interview.

STORY WITH A MORAL

Just as your body, and therefore your mind, is not at peak performance when it is hungry, the same is true when you have eaten too heavy a meal.

I once made the mistake of eating a large meal before my phone interview. I did not want that mid-afternoon hunger to arise during my interview, so I ate a hearty meal of steak and potatoes for lunch. Boy, was I tired for my phone interview an hour later. That food sat in my stomach and wore me out. My body performed at a slow pace, and so did I on my phone interview.

Moral of the Story: Do not let food hinder your phone interview performance. Eat something healthy before your interview to keep your body energized and ready to go.

NATURE RULES

When your body tells you something, you must respond. Your body does not concern itself with whether or not this is an appropriate time to be sick, tired, or, in this case, to go to the restroom. Therefore, you must take care of your physical body regardless of the situation. In order to prevent your body from hindering your phone interview, take care of these things beforehand. Go to the restroom. It is a simple concept, but one that is often forgotten until it is too late.

It does not do you any good if you have the urge to go during your phone interview. This would be distracting and painful. Make sure you answer the call from nature before your phone interview. You do not want to be in discomfort while you are trying to impress your interviewer. You certainly do not want to move your phone interview to the restroom. Flushing is not an appropriate phone interview background noise.

VOICE

Your voice is the only instrument you have during your phone interview to create an action; an action of movement to the next step—a face-to-face interview. Your voice is the key to your phone interview success! You want your voice to be fine-tuned, well-rested, and comparable to a singing bird to the person on the other end of the phone.

Your voice allows you to make a great impression on your interview. You don't want your voice to be shaky from nerves or at an uncomfortable listening pitch or volume. Rather, you want your voice to sound confident, strong, and professional. The way you obtain these three characteristics is by tuning your voice prior to your interview.

How do you determine if you have a professional- and positive-sounding voice? One suggestion is to tape yourself speaking on a voice message or purchase a small tape recorder to listen to your voice.

What feeling do you get when you listen to your own voice? Is it powerful, full of life and energy? If not, don't worry; most people are surprised by the sound of their own voice. Practice talking and listening to yourself to fully develop your phone interview voice.

What are you aiming for? You want your voice to put you in a good light. The goal is for your voice to sound:

- Pleasant.
- Natural.
- Dynamic.
- Expressive.
- Easily heard.
- Strong.
- Confident.
- Professional.

Be sure to let your voice reflect who you are: a professional, strong, eager, and talented individual.

Something to Think About...

Think back to times when you purchased an answering machine or new cell phone. The first thing you need to do is set up your voicemail box. After you set up your voicemail, the machine plays it back so you can hear how it sounds. In all the times you have set up new voicemail boxes, have you ever liked your message on the first try?

Chances are, you recorded it several times before you found a voice tone and speed that sounded pleasant on your voicemail, one that you knew your callers would understand and enjoy. The same applies to your phone interview. You need to practice your voice to find a strong, energetic tone that will convey confidence and professionalism over the telephone.

It takes practice to tone your voice. Practice before your phone interview so that your voice can reflect the perfect job candidate that you are.

Exercise Your Voice Muscles

Successful athletes arrive early to a match in order to stretch and warm up their muscles. They perform best when they have plenty of time to limber up and flex their bodies. This can also be applied to a phone interview. When first waking up, people often need to clear their throat and talk for a few minutes before their voice is clear and they can speak easily. It's also common to have a scratchy voice if you have not spoken in a while. For these reasons, you should be sure to exercise your voice muscles in preparation for your phone interview. You want to be able to speak and enunciate well in order to present yourself in a professional manner.

One hour before your interview, talk to a friend or relative in order to get your voice warmed up. (This is especially important if it's an early-morning phone interview.) Whenever I have an early morning interview, I wake up and talk to my wife. This gets my voice muscles moving and ready for my conversation. If no one will talk to you, turn on the radio while you're getting dressed and sing. Singing will exercise your voice so you can sound clear and confident on your phone interview.

Singing

"La-La-La-La-La!" What better way to start off the day of your phone interview than to sing aloud? It will exercise your voice muscles and pump you up for your interview.

Practice different tones and pitches before your phone interview. Professional speakers exercise their voices before speaking, and so can you. Singing will stretch out your voice muscles and also give you the energy you need to ace your phone interview. Singing also lowers your stress level, leaving you excited and ready for your interview.

Something to Think About...

Have you ever been in a sad, down-and-out mood, when you turn on the radio, one of your favorite tunes comes on? Chances are, your mood immediately improves. You sing along to your favorite lyrics, and suddenly you are that singing star on stage with the audience cheering for you.

Re-create this positive attitude the morning of your phone interview. Rock out to your favorite song to improve your voice performance and your mental outlook. So break out your iPod, download your favorite songs, and get your voice ready to rock! Sound great, feel great—perform like a rock star!

Cough Drop

Who would have thought something as simple as a cough drop can help you get a job? I always take a cough drop before I give a presentation. This almost always eliminates the need to have a glass of water as a quick fix for dry mouth. An hour before your phone interview, take a cough drop—not a Jolly Rancher or a Lifesaver. A cough drop is a small medicated candy intended to be dissolved slowly in the mouth to lubricate and soothe irritated tissues of the throat (usually due to a sore throat), possibly from the common cold or influenza.

Even if you're not ill, a cough drop can positively affect your health—hence potentially improving your performance on the phone interview. You want your cough drop to be a nice, natural, soothing cough drop. Not one of those strong menthol cough drops that make your eyes water from the vapors. If you are opposed to taking a cough drop, you may want to take one tablespoon of all-natural honey to soothe your throat before your phone interview.

Make sure your throat is comfortable and ready to go before your phone interview. This will alleviate the need to drink water during your interview. Imagine you are on the phone with your interviewer and you have a scratchy throat. To keep from clearing your throat, you take a big gulp of water. Now your mouth is full while your interviewer is waiting for a response to his or her last question. You choke on the water, causing you to let out the cough you tried to stifle.

Take a cough drop instead of trying to drink and talk at the same time. Don't click that cough drop around in your mouth or let it impact your speech and voice during your phone interview. Neither of these options results in a pleasant conversation for the person on the other end of the phone.

A cough drop causes your throat to feel refreshed and reduces dryness, so you won't need to cough during your phone interview. This will increase your voice tone and quality. Some cough drops also come with menthol to help you breathe, increasing oxygen intake. A cough drop is a small but helpful way to increase the overall quality of your phone interview.

Take a cough drop or a spoonful of honey before your phone interview. This will soothe your throat, leaving your voice primed and ready to carry on a conversation. Even if you are feeling completely healthy, try these tactics.

Talking for an extended period of time is never easy on your throat. Don't let a scratchy throat take away from the quality of your phone interview.

Breath Produces Voice

The power of your voice comes from breathing. This is a silent process. It is not a process that a person should be able to hear over the phone, especially during a professional call.

Your breathing during your phone interview should be deep, controlled, natural, and even. Of course, you don't need to breathe like you would in a yoga class—you have many other things to concentrate on during your phone interview. However, you do need to be aware of your breathing; you need to feel comfortable, calm your nerves, and speak clearly. You do not want to be winded or out of breath when talking on the phone.

If you are getting stressed before the phone rings, take nice, long breaths. This will give your body more oxygen, which will help you calm down and think clearly.

Remember, breathing is a silent process. You do not want to take a deep loud breath, answer an entire question while holding in that air, and then exhale loudly. This will break up the flow of your interview and cause you to appear nervous and unsure. During your phone interview, be sure to maintain nice, easy breathing.

Something to Think About...

Have you ever watched a horror movie in which the innocent teenage girl answers the phone and the crazy killer is on the other end of the line? How does he talk? He breathes loudly on the phone line, masking his voice and speech.

Have you ever watched a sports match and the announcer interviews the MVP immediately following the game? How does he talk? He is tired from the game and has to take deep breaths after every few words.

These are two examples of breathing getting in the way of voice. In these cases, heavy breathing enhances the role that is being portrayed. However, you are not a horror film character or a star athlete. You are a serious, business-oriented professional. Even, controlled breathing is necessary for this role. Control your breathing during your phone interview. It should be silent and calm, proving you are confident and prepared for this interview.

Find Your Voice

Did you ever notice how many roles you play in your life? Mom/dad, brother/sister, professional, friend, boss, leader—the list goes on. Each of these life roles comes with a set of traits that makes us uniquely qualified to succeed in these roles. One of these qualities is our voice.

If you are in your Dad role, you are an authoritative fig-ure in order to control your children and teach them to behave. However, when you leave that setting to go to the workplace, you may be the subordinate who has to follow rules and regulations. Each role comes with dif-ferent responsibilities.

In addition, each of these roles comes with a different voice tone and feel. Before your phone interview, you must determine which voice you plan to use to be successful and put yourself in the best light for the interviewer. Find your phone interview voice. Becoming aware of your role during the phone interview will allow you to choose the correct voice that will lead you to success.

STORY WITH A MORAL

I can remember having a client who had a very harsh voice, making it difficult to understand what he was saying. His unpleasant voice did not inspire me to keep him on the phone longer than necessary.

This client's voice was not up to the task of a phone interview. I recommended he take singing lessons to improve his speech, voice variety, and his ability to be easily understood. Taking singing lessons improved the tonal quality and strength of his speaking voice while reducing vocal tension and fatigue.

Moral of the Story: Have a pleasant voice that is easy on the ears of the phone interviewer. Turn your voice into action—a face-to-face interview.

Use your voice prior to your phone interview. You may have prepared for days, but if your voice sounds like you just woke up, your interviewer will be under the impression that you are unprofessional and not taking this interview seriously. Do yourself a favor and prepare your voice for victory.

UMS AND AHHS

Ums and *ahhs* are fillers, verbal spaces we use when we talk and are not sure what to say. We use *ums* and *ahhs* as a way to give our brains time to gather thoughts together before speaking.

Often, we do not even notice these fillers in everyday conversation. However, if you are attuned to them, you will realize most people use fillers far too often. On a phone interview, you do not have facial and body expressions to add to the content of your speech. This means fillers are even more apparent. These *ums* and *ahhs* can quickly become very distracting and annoying. The best way to remove *ums* and *ahhs* from your phone interview is to practice. The more you practice, the better you'll be. There are several strategies you can use to remove *ums* and *ahhs* from your speech:

- ✆ Wait for your brain to catch up to your thoughts.
- ✆ Listen, think, and then respond.

- ℂ Relax; don't stress.
- ℂ Bite your tongue.
- ℂ Squeeze your hand.
- ℂ Close your mouth.
- ℂ Take a deep breath.

Do whatever works best for you, but don't use *ums* and *ahhs* during your phone interview. They don't add any value to your phone interview, and won't help you get to the next step. Try to replace *ums* and *ahhs* with a pause. A pause is a sign of intelligence. It means you're thinking before responding to a question; you're not simply reacting.

Something to Think About…

Think back to presentations or lectures you have attended. One or two *uhms* from speakers go pretty much unnoticed. However, if speakers or professors use many *ums* and *ahhs*, it becomes distracting. In fact, if it continues, it may get to the point at which you begin counting fillers rather than listening to content.

How did you feel about these speakers once they had concluded? You most likely did not fully grasp the concepts they were trying to get across. Also, they may have appeared nervous and unprofessional. Do you want these people presenting your work to a team of individuals? No; you want a representative who is going to speak clearly with confidence.

This applies to you and your phone interview. You are representing yourself to the interviewer through your voice. Don't let fillers take away from your content! Present yourself with certainty on your phone interview. Exude confidence by removing all *ums* and *ahhs* from your speech. Don't lose time and value from your phone interview.

SET THE TONE AND PACE OF THE INTERVIEW

You need to determine what type of phone interview you plan to perform before the phone rings. You get to decide this within the first 60 seconds. Plan to influence the interview through your tone and word choice.

There are a few types of phone interviews you need to know to help you manage the phone interview process:

- ℂ Nice and friendly. Go with free-flowing information. This is similar to talking to a long-lost friend. Just be careful not to let your defenses down too much.

- ℂ Dazed and confused. The interviewer is posing questions you didn't prepare for. Make sure you're ready for any and all questions.

- ℂ Fast and furious. Go, go, go! This type of interview is similar to the game 20 Questions—a rapid-fire session.

© Just the facts. Follow the five Ws regarding your professional experience (who, what, where, when, and why). Just use your resume as a guide and take it from the top.

© FBI Special. Question after question after question. They want the answer—nothing more and nothing less. Give them what they want—and fast. Time is of the essence, and they're evaluating how you think and work under pressure.

© Clueless. You must be both interviewee and interviewer. The person on the other end of the phone may not be able to handle a professional phone interview. You must take control and make the best of the situation.

You need to determine what will work best for you and the interviewer. At times, you may choose to use a few of these techniques, depending on the question and phase of the phone interview.

Remember that each phone interview is unique. Is your interview going to be friendly, warm, and open? Or is it going to be very direct, harsh, and emotionally draining? You need to decide what the tone of your interview will be.

Something to Think About...

Remember that every interviewer is different; you cannot choose a particular tone and pace and apply it to all of your phone interviews. Think of how many different types of conversations you carry on each day. For example, you may choose a calm, slow speech to talk to an elderly person, whereas you would convey the same information in a stern, loud voice to your teenager.

Every conversation you have has varying elements. Determine the type of phone interview conversation your interviewer prefers during your phone interview handshake. This will allow you to apply the correct tone and pace to your interview, creating an open and comfortable environment.

In your everyday life, you encounter various people and adapt your conversation accordingly. Do the same on your phone interview to create a positive connection with your interviewer. Set the tone as soon as you pick up the phone!

DRESS UP LIKE YOU WOULD FACE-TO-FACE

Even though the interviewer cannot actually see you on your phone interview, you should still dress for success! This will affect your attitude and emotions during your interview. If you look professional, you will feel and act professional.

You do not want to conduct your phone interview in your pajamas, flip-flops, or summer shorts. If you're dressed for the beach, you will act like you're at the beach. This doesn't put you in the correct frame of mind for a phone interview.

Wearing business attire will pump you up for your phone interview—giving you confidence that you can conquer the world! You will feel more secure in your responses, and the interviewer will notice this through your steady speech and lack of hesitation. He may not be able to see what you are wearing, but he can detect your level of self-assurance. Don't forget to dress to impress!

Something to Think About...

It is a lot of work to get dressed up, but it pays significant dividends. When my son, Connor, wears his Little League baseball uniform, he feels like and believes he is a world champion. When children dress like Superman for Halloween, they think they can fly. When they dress the part, they feel and act the part.

The same applies to your phone interview. If you wear your pajamas and your pink fuzzy slippers, you feel casual, and therefore you will think and act casually. This is not what you want for your phone interview. You must dress professionally in order to take on the role of a powerful, confident businessperson. Simply by dressing the part, you will dramatically increase your performance on your phone interview. Dress to impress and dress for success.

5

MAKE AN IMPRESSION

Timing is everything, even when it comes to your phone interview. You want to make sure your actions and behaviors are timed and coordinated flawlessly to ensure your phone interview success.

WAIT A BEAT

When should you pick up the phone for your phone interview? Should you sit in front of the phone and the moment it makes a sound, pounce on it? Or should you be wandering around the house and casually approach the phone right before it goes to voicemail? Our research has indicated that the second or third rings are the optimum time to answer the phone and begin your interview.

If you answer the phone on the first ring, this may indicate to the interviewer that you're too eager. Just by answering the phone too quickly, the interviewer knows that you're likely to jump at anything your told. This may seem like a positive quality, but in general terms, most people want what they cannot have. For this reason, you do not want to appear too eager.

So why not wait until the fourth ring? By the time the phone rings a fourth time, you have missed your opportunity. You appear careless and unprepared for the phone interview. If you do miss the second and third rings, let the call go to voicemail.

Once the interviewer has left a message, take a deep breath, and get your story straight as to why you did not pick up the phone. Then immediately call back. Briefly explain your excuse and get right into the interview. You do not want to waste time apologizing. Excel at the rest of your interview, and your missed call in the beginning will quickly be forgotten.

People conducting phone interviews are expecting you to answer the phone on either the second or the third ring. Picking up the phone at this time will show you are both confident and excited about your interview.

Let the phone ring once or twice, take a breath to calm your nerves, and begin.

STORY WITH A MORAL

When my sister started dating, my father taught her a valuable lesson: Never answer a boy's phone call on the first ring lest she appear too eager. No one wants to date someone who is overly excited about the possibility of a new relationship. My father taught her to wait for the second or third ring, and let the boy sweat it out a little (but not too long) before answering the phone. This proved she was interested, but not too readily available.

The same applies to your phone interview. If you jump to answer the phone halfway through the first ring, you appear too eager. You are overly excited and not prepared to begin a calm and intelligent conversation. No one wants to hire someone who is too readily available for the position. Answering the phone for your phone interview on the first ring makes you look nervous and anxious.

Moral of the story: Do what my sister did—use that first ring to take a quick second, calm your nerves, and answer the phone on the second or third ring with a calm and confident mindset.

START WITH HELLO

"Hey Paul!" This is what my high-school buddy Pat says when we get together to watch the Red Sox game. This is very friendly, but it is not the formal greeting you need to use in a business environment.

Start your phone interview off on the right foot with a professional *hello*. Whenever you are answering phone calls regarding your job campaign, you must pick up the receiver and present yourself with a clear and confident hello.

"Hi" is a casual greeting that is used for informal settings, such as greeting an old friend or family members, or talking to a child. On the opposite side of the spectrum, answering the phone with a harsh "[Your name] speaking" is also not appropriate for a phone call pertaining to your job campaign. This greeting is abrupt and impersonal.

"Hello" is the best greeting with which to begin your phone interview. This term presents you as a kind, warm, professional individual. During your next few phone calls, take notice of the way different people greet you. Typically, friends will say *hi*, whereas business professionals will say *hello*. Use the correct greeting to impress your interviewer right from the start.

Something to Think About...

Have you ever taken a foreign language? Think back to your high school or college courses. What was the first thing your professor taught you when learning a new language? The difference between formal and informal expressions.

There are different verb endings and different words altogether, depending on who you are addressing. This is heavily stressed when learning a foreign language—you do not want to insult someone by using improper greetings.

The same applies to English. We may not notice how important it is to know the difference between formal and informal greetings because we have been using them since we were children. However, now is the time to pay attention. Formal greetings, such as *hello*, need to be used in all formal situations when talking to people of authority or power.

This applies to your phone interview. Your interviewer is someone who should be respected and spoken to in a formal manner. Using *hello* is the best way to convey this respect. It is a simple concept, but one that must not be overlooked. The term you use when picking up that receiver is the first thing your interviewer will hear. It is her very first glimpse at the person you are. Make it impressive with a confident, professional *hello*.

PHONE INTERVIEW HANDSHAKE

One of the most important components to a phone interview is the phone handshake. Even though you don't get the opportunity to look the person in the eyes and shake hands, a phone interview handshake can be just as effective. This is a way to get to know the person before the formal part of the interview takes place. It's also a way to establish a rapport with the interviewer before she actually starts asking questions.

What should you do and say during your phone interview handshake?

1. Greeting. "Hello, how are you, [insert name]? I see from your area code you are from Boston. Did you see the Red Sox beat the Yankees yesterday?" Or, "I see in your area the weather is beautiful today." Or, "How are things going for you? I see your company has made the front page today."

2. Length of the greeting. The phone interview handshake should last no more than one and a half minutes. Less is okay, but any longer may indicate that you're not focused and therefore not serious about obtaining the position.

3. Contract. During this greeting period, you want to confirm the agreed upon and allocated

time for the phone interview and also confirm the position for which you are interviewing.

4. Environment. Create a friendly, open, and positive environment during the phone interview handshake. Be humble, upbeat, positive, enthusiastic, respectful, polite, and, most importantly, be yourself.

5. Learn your interviewer's ways. Pay attention to the way your interviewer acts during the phone interview handshake. This will allow you to determine some of his personality traits (friendly, analytical, laid back). You can use this information to strengthen your interaction during your interview.

Your phone interview handshake will determine the path of your entire phone interview. Your interview can go one of two ways. The desired direction is path A. In this scenario, you hit it off well with your interviewer within the first 15 seconds. If you can create this instant connection, your phone interview will be very engaging and meaningful, and great progress will come from your interview.

The other direction is path B. In this scenario, the first 15 seconds of your phone interview handshake are awkward and unsteady. Unfortunately, this will ultimately result in a non-engaging, stale, robotic phone interview. If you do not establish a good connection with your interviewer within the first 15 seconds of your phone interview, your interview will most likely be unsuccessful.

Make sure your phone interview is headed down path A with a great phone interview handshake—personable, professional, and polite. A positive foundation created within the first 15 seconds will steer your conversation and your phone interview toward the next steps in your interview process.

STORY WITH A MORAL

I was conducting a phone interview for a team manager position. The candidate was very knowledgeable and skilled, and had great educational background, but she was not personable. When she picked up the phone, she immediately wanted to jump into the interview. She told me, "It is great to meet you, let's jump into the interview so we do not waste any time," which made it very difficult for me to relate to her.

This was a driven, business-oriented individual, but she was not personable. Because she neglected the phone interview handshake, I got the feeling she was not very sociable. She did not create an open, friendly environment at the beginning of the phone interview, which made me question her ability to create this kind of positive work environment as a leader of a team project.

Moral of the Story: Begin your phone interview with a phone interview handshake. This demonstrates your friendly, personable nature. It allows you to connect with your interviewer, displaying your ability to create positive interactions among individuals in a business-oriented setting. Start your interview with the phone interview handshake!

CONVERSATION

A phone interview is a conversation. It's not a debate. It's not a question and answer session. It's not a trial. It's not an inquisition.

A conversation is an exchange of information between two or more people. A conversation allows people to learn from each other. A phone interview is not a one-sided conversation in which one person speaks and the other person stays quiet. Be prepared for a conversation so you can add value to the exchange of information.

You want to uphold your end of the conversation. You want to be able to add value to the discussion by educating the other party about yourself and what you can bring to the organization. On the opposite side of the table, you want to engage the person who is interviewing you—sharing and adding to the overall conversation. In this way, both parties will have a positive experience.

For practice, conduct your own phone interview; play the parts of both the interviewer and the interviewee (you). Create your own scenarios, build your comfort level, and even practice telling stories that will give the interviewer a glimpse into the real you. Practice, as always, is a big part of this. Do your homework; practice your interview.

Something to Think About...

Think of a time when you were at a dinner party or networking event with a large number of people. There is typically time to mingle, converse, and get to know the other people in attendance. Sometimes you have excellent conversations, and other times it is awkward and uncomfortable.

What goes wrong with these conversations that you are quickly looking for an exit strategy? There are several possibilities.

First, the other individual may be bombarding you with questions; as soon as you answer one, she is right back with another question. There is no discussion. This can make you feel like you are on the hot seat at a trial. This is not a pleasurable conversation.

On the opposite side of the spectrum, the other person may not be saying much of anything at all. He may simply nod and respond "uh huh" to whatever you say. This is a one-sided conversation that makes you feel the listener is bored by what you are saying. No one wants to talk to someone who is not bringing anything to the discussion.

In both these examples, the other individuals appear to lack a key social ingredient—confidence. They are forcing you to carry the conversation. These are not the types of people you want to socialize with at the dinner party.

Be the person with whom everyone wants to converse—at the networking event and on your phone interview. Listen intently and then bring your own thoughts and opinions to the discussion. Add value to create a conversation, and add conversation to create a valuable phone interview.

ATTITUDE IS KEY

An attitude is a hypothetical concept that represents an individual's degree of like or dislike for an item. Attitudes are generally positive or negative views of a person, place, thing, or event—this is often referred to as the attitude object.

Your attitude is a key factor in the success of your phone interview. This is in your control. You get to decide if you are going to be positive or negative during your interview. Undoubtedly, you want to appear excited about this opportunity; a negative outlook will be portrayed through your responses, and your hiring appeal will diminish.

There are many activities you can do in order to mentally prepare for your phone interview:

- ✆ Read the newspaper.
- ✆ Listen to music.
- ✆ Watch an inspirational show.
- ✆ Talk and laugh with a friend about good things.
- ✆ Think good thoughts.
- ✆ Eat something you enjoy (but not too much before your interview because you don't want to get tired).
- ✆ Exercise to release stress.

Staying positive and energized throughout your interview will give you the drive to answer questions with enthusiasm. Positive attitudes are also contagious. Have you ever noticed how one excited person can make a whole group of people excited? Conversely, one negative person with a list of complaints often provokes others to complain. Take the time before your phone interview to make sure you get in the zone and exude a positive attitude!

Something to Think About...

Think of a time when your attitude affected your mood during a situation. For example, imagine you are invited to your colleague's birthday party. It is a far drive and you know you are going to be exhausted from the many work meetings you have earlier that day, but she is a nice person, so you decide the right thing to do would be to attend.

Now you are at the party and you are constantly checking your watch. How long do you need to stay before it is no longer inappropriate to leave? No one at the party is interacting with you because they can sense that your attitude of begrudging attendance does not match theirs of genuine enthusiasm. You did not want to come to the party and so now your mind is already made up that you are not going to have a good time.

Do not let this happen on your phone interview. You need to have a positive attitude going into the interview. You have to want to talk to this person about this job opportunity. If you are not focused and excited, your interviewer, just like the fellow partygoers, will not be interested in talking to you. You need to demonstrate enthusiasm, as this positivity will carry over into your conversation and phone interview environment.

Go into your phone interview with a positive attitude. Put all negative thoughts out of your mind and focus on the task at hand. If you're happy about your interview, your interviewer will be too!

ETIQUETTE

Etiquette is defined as "the customary code of polite behavior in society or among members of a particular profession or group." This includes the unwritten rules that influence expectations for social behavior. Good etiquette is necessary whenever you are interacting with other people, so of course, it's necessary for a successful phone interview. You must do what is expected of you without being told. This includes:

- No gum chewing.
- No nail biting.
- No mumbling.
- No candy in your mouth.
- No burping.
- No yawning.

Basically, don't do anything on a phone interview that you wouldn't do at a face-to-face interview. Just because the interviewer cannot see that pile of Jolly Ranchers, he or she can still hear it clicking around in your mouth. If you present polite behavior on your phone interview, the interviewer will believe you complete all tasks with this same respect and professionalism. This is an important impression you must leave with the interviewer in order to achieve the desired position.

Something to Think About...

I was walking through the halls of my high school, Archbishop Molloy High School, in Queens, New York, during school hours. I was asked to give a presentation to the juniors and seniors for Career Day. I stopped to talk to one of the students and he was chewing a piece of gum. This chomping is not conducive to conversation, as it gets in the way of speech, not to mention it makes an awfully annoying sound. This gum chewing needs to stay in the hallways of ninth grade. It should not be carried out in your phone interview. It is unprofessional and disrespectful to your listener.

Spit out your gum and dispose of all other impolite habits for your phone interview. Carry yourself with great social etiquette and your interviewer will see you as a professional, respectful person.

Be Earnest

An earnest person is defined as someone who is "serious in intention, purpose, or effort; someone who shows depth and sincerity of feeling." This characteristic exemplifies the ideal candidate for phone interviews. You don't want to come as though like you think you're too good for this position and already know everything. You also don't want to appear to be a complete nervous wreck. You must find the happy medium. This middle ground is best represented by being earnest. Display a serious attitude about the position for which you are interviewing. Listen intently and respond with answers that show you are genuinely interested in the job.

If you are earnest during your phone interview, it is implied that you are also an earnest worker. This creates a trusting atmosphere between you and your potential employer.

Something to Think About...

Think back to a conversation you had when first meeting someone. Could you tell how he felt about meeting you right off the bat? Of course you could. You can tell when someone is excited to be talking to you and when he is just trying to find an exit strategy.

You can tell when people are purely acting during a conversation. They're pompous or simply ignoring what you are saying. These are not people with whom you will be inclined to carry on a second conversation.

The same applies to phone interviewing. On a phone interview, not only can your interviewer tell you are faking it the same way she can during a face-to-face conversation, but it is even more obvious when she has only voice to characterize a person. Your voice is all the interviewer has to work with, and so a lack of sincerity is even more apparent over the telephone. Be earnest during your phone interview. Be sincere and respectful. This will come through in your voice when speaking with your interviewer.

BE HUMBLE

What does it mean to be humble? Respect the interviewer, do not be aggressive, and remember, you are working to serve this company, to help it grow and prosper.

During your phone interview, make sure your ego is always in check. This means you must exhibit your value proposition (what value you bring to the organization) in a passive, but still powerful manner. Don't let your ego get in the way of the positive content of your phone interview.

People respect individuals who can put others first. This demonstrates they are team players, working for the greater good rather than personal advantage. Reflect the personality trait of being humble. We all have egos that need to be boosted through compliments and praise, but your phone interview is not the time to advance your ego. During your phone interview you need to be kind—check your ego at the door.

Something to Think About...

What would your reaction be if you were looking to hire someone and, when you called him on the telephone, he immediately began with "I am great, I am perfect for this job, when are you going to hire me?" Chances are, you are probably going to look into additional candidates, because this individual has a big ego. How will he work with others if he always acts like he knows best?

Don't be this person on your phone interview. Be humble—show you are an intelligent individual who is open to new ideas and strategies. This will impress your interviewers and increase their desire to talk more with you about the position.

LAUGHTER

It is important to realize that it is okay to laugh during your phone interview. Just make sure that it is appropriate. If your interview is going well, meaning it has been professional and value-oriented, it will not take away from your performance to give a small laugh at a humorous comment.

Of course, you do not want to laugh the entire time. This would demonstrate a lack of seriousness and respect.

On the other end of the spectrum, if you are too stiff and serious, the interviewer may feel you are too cold to work well with a team. You want to find the happy medium.

If you and the interviewer are connecting and someone shares a story, it is okay to laugh. It shows you are human and have a personality. Showing a good sense of humor implies you are a kind, friendly individual. This is a positive quality to have during the interview process. Being able to laugh in your interview will make your discussion more of a conversation, easing tensions on both ends of the phone line. If you are having a good time, your interviewer will, too.

Story With a Moral

When giving a presentation, I typically try to keep the audience's interest by telling a few small jokes related to the subject. Once, I was giving a presentation, and when I made a joke, no one in the audience laughed. They were all writing down every word I said, too serious to realize I was trying to make the presentation fun and interesting.

This made me feel awkward and certainly did not loosen any tension in the room. It also did not make me feel like I wanted to have a conversation with any of these people after the presentation because they seemed too stiff and even came off a bit standoffish. Don't let these negative personality traits come across in your phone interview.

Moral of the Story: Be on topic, be professional, but also be human. If something is funny, laugh. It shows you are a friendly, open person. This will help build a connection with your interviewer and bring a pleasant atmosphere to your phone interview.

STAY FOCUSED—DON'T MULTITASK

It is difficult to pay attention during phone interviews because the person with whom you are speaking is not sitting in front of you. Because the interviewer cannot see you, you may think you can get away with glancing around the room and fidgeting with objects on your desk while on the phone. This isn't true. You must remain completely focused on your interview; don't try to multitask. Missing one statement made by the interviewer could have detrimental effects on your chances of acquiring the position. Such multitasking might include:

- ✆ Surfing the Web or playing computer games.

- ✆ Clicking your mouse repetitively.

- ✆ Playing with items around you.

If you feel you are easily distracted and drawn to multitasking, remove or turn off anything you might be tempted to use. It is necessary that you remain focused! You must listen carefully so you can respond professionally and to the point.

Story With a Moral

People always have a lot of things to do when they are at work. I often have several simultaneous projects. We, as busy human beings, try to increase our productivity by doing more than one task at once. However, this can backfire.

I once was waiting for a document that laid out project expenses, which needed to be confirmed before we could begin the task at hand. Well, the person on the other end of this transaction must have been multitasking at his desk, because I received a letter of appreciation for a donation, addressed to a different company! This person had mixed up the envelopes and mailed the wrong mail to the wrong parties. This only slowed down our process and also did not make the sender look efficient or organized.

Moral of the Story: Stay focused on your phone interview. Invest the time in acing your interview, and then you can move on to the next project. Multitasking makes mistakes!

Talk to a Photograph

Speaking to a photograph during your phone interview gives you the feeling of talking to another person. This will make your interview more natural and realistic. If the person you are meeting on your phone interview has a LinkedIn profile with a professional photo, print it out and look at it during your interview. This will improve your presentation, as you will be able to connect with your interviewer through what feels similar to a face-to-face interview.

If you cannot access a photograph of your interviewer, pick an influential, professional leader. You can write to the United States president asking for an autographed photo. Take this photo and frame it so you can look at it during your phone interview.

Speaking to a powerful individual will help to make your presentation more professional. It also develops your ability to have a serious, business-oriented conversation without the added pressure of an actual face-to-face interaction. This will help prepare you for future interviews.

You should be sitting down during your phone interview. Walking around and talking on the phone is not an appropriate manner to impress someone on a phone interview because it's unnatural, and can be distracting to you if your frame of vision is constantly changing. You wouldn't pace back and forth for a face-to-face interview, so don't do it now. Imagine this is a face-to-face with your influential photograph.

Another common mistake is looking at yourself in the mirror. It's often thought that this is an appropriate strategy to pretend you can see the person you are on the phone with, but this actually causes you to become focused on your reflection and not on the interview. This is also very unnatural. Looking in the mirror is also a problem because it encourages you to smile all the time. This is not appropriate for your phone interview. You do not naturally smile when you speak, so do not do it while on the phone. It will affect your voice, making your speech sound unnatural.

Talking to a photograph may make you feel silly, but it's actually an effective technique when participating in a phone interview. It increases your performance level and thus your chances of obtaining the position.

Something to Think About...

Imagine you are sitting in front of the president of the United States in the oval office. You probably feel pretty important, right? You are certainly in a professional mindset. Now imagine you are sitting across from your kids at the beach. You feel relaxed, laid back, and are using vocabulary at the level of a first-grade student.

The attitude that you have when you imagine yourself sitting in front of the president is the attitude you want to have during your phone interview. To make it easier to get into this mindset, set the scene! Have a photograph of your interviewer or an influential person set up where you are conducting your phone interview to make you feel serious, powerful, and professional.

Keep Track of Time

One benefit to phone interviews as opposed to face-to-face interviews is that it is not rude to look at the time. Use this to your advantage! Have a clock in the room where you are conducting your phone interview so you can keep track of the time. Make sure this clock is visible during your phone interview. You do not want to be distracted by trying to flip your watch over on your wrist or pushing papers aside in order to see the time. A quick glance should be all you need in order to ensure you're on track.

Also, make sure this clock has no buzzers or alarms. Such a sound would not only be incredibly disruptive to your thought process, but would also create background noise that would sound unprofessional to the interviewer.

The goal of keeping track of time is to use it efficiently and effectively. Let no minute pass during your phone interview that is not being leveraged to send the message that you are a perfect candidate for this opportunity and the reasons why.

Evenly space your time by mapping out your interview. This allows for a smooth process and subtracts from the stresses of any job interview.

There are three key parts to your phone interview: Beginning, Middle, and End, or, as I like to call it, ICC— Introduction, Conducting, and Conclusion. You need to make sure you will have time for all three. In each section, you need to make key points concerning the value you will bring to the company. Incorporating this into all three parts of your phone interview will instill your positive, professional image in the interviewer's mind.

The majority of your time during your phone interview needs to be spent on the middle, or the conduction. Here is an example of what you might consider a successful time schedule:

© First 15 seconds: These seconds will make or break your phone interview. They are extremely important. Make sure your voice is pleasant, as it will be the first impression you make on the interviewer.

℃ 16 seconds to one minute and 45 seconds later:
The phone interview handshake. Get connected with your interviewer on a human level.
Brief small talk will ease your nerves and lead
to a better phone conversation. This is when
you want to confirm the allotted time for your
phone interview. Here is an example of an eloquent way to do this: "Ms. Jones, I know you
are very busy and I appreciate you sharing your
time with me today. I want to confirm that we
have one hour to spend together on the phone
and so we will go from 1:00 to 2:00. I have
another appointment at 2:00." Remember, you
always have another appointment because you
are busy and in demand. You have no time to
waste.

℃ Next 50 minutes: Conducting your phone interview. The key message here is to remember
people hire people for two reasons: to make
the organization money and to save the organization money. Remember to keep this
in mind when you are telling the interviewer
about all your positive attributes and how the
company will benefit from your employment.

© Final 8 minutes: Concluding your interview. This is when you want to ask your knockout questions. It is also the time when you want to be sure to say, "Ms. Jones, if I have any additional questions, can I reach out to you?" The interviewer will almost always say yes. This will allow you to send the company article you obtained during your preparation research, proving your professionalism and intelligence.

The key item to remember when keeping track of time is to *never* go over the previously allotted time for your phone interview, no matter how great the interview is going.

Story With a Moral

My friend had a phone interview for a senior position as a plant manager for a large automobile company. He was a perfect fit for the job—great education in the field, great background experience, and he was well-prepared for his phone interview.

His phone interview was going so well that a one-hour interview turned into an hour and a half. Sounds like everything was going great, right? As my friend continued, the conversation passed the designated stop time and the hiring manager thought to himself, "If this person cannot stick to the allocated time in a phone interview, how is he going to manage a production schedule of an automobile plant?" My friend did not get this job.

Moral of the Story: Map out your time during your phone interview. Stick to the scheduled time session to prove your professionalism and time management skills. Having a planned timeline will decrease your stress, allowing you to space your discussion evenly, resulting in a better phone interview performance. During the phone interview, time is on your side.

THE 15-MINUTE RULE

We have all heard of the five-minute rule when someone screams "Time!" before leaving their position in a family-friendly football game. This allows the players to rest and drink water before resuming the game. Well, this is the 15-minute phone interview rule.

If your interviewer was scheduled to call at 1 p.m. and at 1:15 p.m. he still has not called, you have waited long enough for your scheduled phone interview. Do not answer the phone if your interviewer calls more than 15 minutes later than scheduled. Why? Your time is valuable. You do not have time to sit around waiting for a phone call all afternoon.

If you answer the phone at 1:30 p.m. when the interviewer finally calls, it appears you have been waiting around all afternoon for the phone call. This gives the impression that you have nothing else to do. You appear inactive and too readily available. No one wants to hire an individual who is always too eager, nor do they want to hire someone who appears lazy.

How do you handle this situation? When the interviewer calls, let him or her leave a message. Then, wait an hour and call back. Say something such as, "Hello Mr. Jones, I'm sorry I missed your call. I understood we were going to begin our phone conversation at one o'clock, but when it reached 1:15, I assumed something had come up and I took an international call. Unfortunately, I am booked for this afternoon, but I would be interested in rescheduling our phone interview. When is good for you?"

You do not want to attack your interviewer about being late, but you do want him to know you were prepared at the scheduled time. However, you are also an individual in high demand. You have other responsibilities and your time is valuable. Following the 15-minute phone interview rule will determine your interviewer's first impression of you. Make your interviewer believe you are a driven, goal-based individual by handling late calls with proper phone interview etiquette.

STORY WITH A MORAL

When I was in school, this same rule applied to a professor's attendance in class. If the professor was more than 15 minutes late, the students were allowed to leave the classroom without penalty of skipping if the professor showed up later than the scheduled lecture time.

One time when this happened, a friend of mine and I decided to stay in our seats, thinking the professor would think positively of us if we waited passed the required wait time. When our professor arrived 45 minutes late, he was shocked to see us still in attendance. However, to our surprise, he was not impressed to see us still waiting.

"Why did you wait 45 minutes for me? I would think bright students would have realized something had come up and left after 15 minutes to do something productive with their time."

Our plan had completely backfired. Our professor did not think of us as dedicated students. Rather, we gave the impression of being lazy individuals.

Moral of the Story: Don't let this happen to you during your phone interview. Follow the 15-minute rule to prove you are a professional and productive individual. Prove your time is valuable.

TAKE NOTES

Before your phone interview begins, gather at least two pens or pencils and some paper. Put them where they are easily accessible so that you can take notes. Make sure you have more than one writing utensil (as pens can run out of ink and pencil tips can break), and more than one piece of paper so you can keep your notes organized.

Do not take notes on a computer or laptop. This could be harmful to your interview for several reasons:

© Clicking noises can be heard as background noise, and that's generally unprofessional and distracting to the interviewer.

© Computers crash and laptop batteries die. This could leave you unable to take notes, and of course, you could lose all the notes you had taken in the beginning.

Even if you have no other windows open, computers offer a number of distractions, such as pop-ups and screensavers.

Stick to old-fashioned hand-written notes during your phone interview.

Write down what you were asked and how you responded. Make sure to print legibly so you can read them later, but don't spend so much time writing every word down that you lose the conversational aspect of the phone interview.

Take short notes during your phone interview, and then rewrite them with longer explanations afterward so you can understand your notes and use them for a reference in the future.

STORY WITH A MORAL

When I attend classes or lectures, I always bring a paper and pen to take notes. Once I made the mistake of sitting next to someone who was taking notes on her laptop. The constant clicking of her fingers on the keys was extremely annoying and distracting. I suppose it was distracting to her as well because she had to ask me numerous times to look at my notes because she missed what the speaker said.

Taking notes on a laptop was not beneficial to this person, nor was it beneficial to the people around her. This can also be applied to your phone interview. Taking notes the old-fashioned way is the best way to pay attention and also capture information for later review.

Moral of the Story: Taking notes should never be a distraction; it should be a helpful tool. Avoid problems associated with your note-taking by legibly printing short, understandable notes using paper and a pen during your phone interview.

Relax and Have Fun!

A phone interview is not meant to be frightening in the sense that you are staring at the phone, dreading the moment it rings. Of course, you need to be thinking on your toes, but this doesn't mean your palms should be sweating or your voice shaking. Relax! The person on the other end of the phone is simply that—a person. She wants to hire and meet new employees just as much as you want to be hired and meet new employers.

Before your phone interview begins, do not sit at your desk, watching the clock, and timing the racing speed of your pulse. Instead, take a few moments to calm down and relax. There are several ways you can calm your nerves:

- ℭ Close your eyes and think happy thoughts.
- ℭ Concentrate on your breathing. Conduct breathing exercises.
- ℭ Walk, run, or exercise.
- ℭ Tell yourself "I can do this."

These are just a few examples of ways to release the stomach butterflies while you practice being comfortable in your own skin.

A phone interview is a chance to meet a new person, create a new network, and discover new job opportunities that can be very exciting. If you have fun on your phone interview, the interviewer will do the same.

Something to Think About...

Think of a time when you were meeting a bunch of new people for the first time. Maybe it was move-in day at college or your first day at a new job. You were probably nervous to meet these new people. When you are nervous, you are tense and acting unnaturally. These people are not meeting the real you, or you at your best.

After a few days, you become more comfortable around these people and are no longer anxious to make a good impression during your encounters. Now that you are no longer putting up a front, you are presenting a more positive, valuable individual than before—you are portraying your true self.

This can also be applied to your phone interview. You are nervous and trying to conform to the person you think the interviewer wants you to be. You do not need to do this. Simply be yourself and the interviewer will be able to see the energetic, professional individual you naturally are.

You have prepared, you have practiced, you are ready. There is no need to stress. Relax and have a good time. You'll be great!

6

WORLD-CLASS PHONE INTERVIEW IN ACTION

You deserve a better opportunity, and all you need to do is get past the phone interview. The following techniques will assist you in being a champion phone interviewee. Make it happen!

IT'S IN YOUR CONTROL

The interviewer may be asking the questions, but ultimately, you control your phone interview. Don't let anyone take that away from you. You get to decide what you want to happen and how during your phone interview.

In order to maintain control, you must be strong-minded, ruthless, and unwavering. Your responses to questions—how you sound and what you say—is in your control. Imagine what you want the end results of your phone interview to be—what you want the interviewer to take away from this exchange—then focus your control to achieve these goals.

It is all about control, staying in control before, during, and after your phone interview.

Something to Think About...

Have you ever been in a team huddle at a sports match? There's 30 seconds to go, you're down by three, and you need that last great touchdown. What does the coach tell you to do? Don't worry about what the other team is doing. You are on the offense, so worry about yourself.

My coach always used to tell us to focus on our own play. Know the play you are running like the back of your hand, and then it won't matter what the other side does. You know what you are doing and that is what matters. You are in control of this victory.

The same theory can be applied to your phone interview. If you know what you are doing, and have prepared and practiced prior to this interview, you are going to be great. Focus on that end zone and reaching your goal successfully. You are in control of your phone interview victory.

Stay in control. This will give you the confidence and drive you need to ace your phone interview. Success is in your own hands. It's all up to you.

Listen Carefully

Has anyone ever told you the famous saying, "God gave us two ears and one mouth so we could listen more and talk less"? This is wise advice that should definitely be applied to your phone interview.

Listen, listen, listen. Don't just hear, but listen. There is a significant difference between the two. To listen is not only to be physically present, but to give your full attention to the speaker. Your entire mind, body, and soul should be focused on the information being presented. Do not just hear the words, but use deep, intellectual thinking to process what the speaker is saying. Listening means there are no distractions. Do not try to jump to a point or anticipate the next words. Just be present. Listen to how the interviewer is speaking, listen for understanding, listen to the meaning, listen for the unspoken words. This active concentration is what you need to do during your phone interview.

How do you demonstrate you are listening when you are on the phone? The interviewer cannot see your head nodding or focused gaze; therefore, offer a subtle "I understand" or "Yes, good point" to show you are listening intently.

The real proof of your listening is in your response to the interviewer's questions. The more in-depth and analytical the answer, the greater the demonstration that you are listening and, most importantly, understanding what the interviewer is saying. Understanding is the key to true listening. And this mutual understanding creates a strong connection between yourself and the interviewer.

Do not assume that you must talk more on your phone interview to make the best impression. Everybody loves to talk, but only a few people like to listen. Don't worry—you will have your opportunity to talk. Be sure to also take full advantage of your opportunity to listen.

Something to Think About...

Think back to a time when it was required for you to attend a meeting or a lecture and you just did not want to go. Maybe you had other things to do, a lot on your mind, or you needed the time to be doing something else.

So what happened? You attended the event, but with only half your brain. With the other half, you were making weekend plans, thinking about upcoming deadlines, or trying to remember if you turned off the coffee pot that morning. You were sitting in the meeting, so it appeared you were paying attention, but in reality, your mind was elsewhere. You heard the words coming out of the speaker's mouth, but you did not internalize them.

You were not making connections between sentences, so the different points were not becoming apparent in your mind.

After the event, someone asked you your thoughts on a particular part and, although you could call up the words that were used because your brain subconsciously stored them, you could not logically analyze them. This is what happens when you hear, but do not listen.

Listening is an active experience. You cannot sit idly by and expect knowledge to just make sense of itself in your brain. You may think it is even easier to pretend to listen on the phone because the speaker cannot see you. Do not be mistaken—active listening is a must for your phone interview. When you are listening, be silent—don't be absent!

DON'T INTERRUPT!

During your phone interview, it is important that you listen closely and do not interrupt. Speaking before your interviewer has finished his or her statement is rude and unprofessional. This implies that you are not listening. Interrupting also suggests you do not value the interviewer's thoughts and believe your ideas are more important.

This is not the attitude you want to portray on your phone interview. Your phone interview needs to be a conversation in which both sides bring valuable thoughts to the table. You must listen and respond accordingly. Do not try to dominate the conversation by interrupting.

Show respect for your interviewer by acknowledging her thoughts by silently listening. Remember, she already has a job in this company, at this particular time, so she has the upper hand. Her knowledge is already accredited by the corporation. Be respectful by pausing after her comments and then speaking your own intelligent response.

By not interrupting, you prove yourself capable of working well with a team of individuals. This also demonstrates an open-minded attitude that is essential for professional conversations. Not only are you showing respect for your interviewer's ideas, but you are also displaying confidence in your own thoughts by inserting them at appropriate times during your phone interview.

Something to Think About...

I have a friend who is very impatient. Often, when I am explaining something to her, she will interrupt, exclaiming, "Yes, okay, I get it." This is extremely irritating, as I am trying to help my friend, yet she interrupts as if she knows better than me.

I am sure you have encountered similar scenarios in your everyday life. Do not let this happen during your phone interview. You do not want to portray yourself as arrogant or rude.

Let your interviewer speak, pause, and then respond. Allowing the conversation to flow smoothly back and forth between speakers will make for a positive phone interview. Respect your interviewer, and respect yourself: Don't interrupt!

THERE IS NO NEED TO RUSH

Do not speak too quickly or frantically during your phone interview. Talking like this will not result in a comfortable conversation and will certainly not impress your interviewer.

Speak clearly and calmly. This resonates that you are a professional, skilled individual who is well-versed in business interactions. You do not want to fill up the air space with rambling words. Instead, present your interviewer with clear, thought-out information that displays your professional presentation skills.

The idea here is quality, not quantity. It does not matter how many words you can fit into the time allotted for your phone interview. What matters is how much content you can get across to your interviewer. Pace your speech evenly, in a well-orchestrated manner, to achieve a top-notch interview.

If you listen to radio or television news broadcasters, you will notice that they speak slowly and very precisely. They do not talk to fill the air with words, but rather use decisive words to clearly explain what they are speaking about.

These professionals know how to enunciate slowly and calmly so they can be understood. You want to conduct your phone interview in the same manner. If you rush, the interviewer will feel you are in a hurry. Maybe you have something you consider more important to do, or maybe you are nervous or unprofessional. None of these are desirable traits to portray during your phone interview.

Be in control, don't rush, and speak deliberately and confidently. Show your phone interviewer the professional, valuable job candidate that you are.

Something to Think About...

Have you ever been in a big hurry and, by rushing, actually made more work for yourself? You dash out the door to get to the store before it closes and, upon arriving, realize you forgot your wallet? You are late for a meeting so you double the speed limit, and, not only do those red and blue flashing lights that pull up behind you make you even later for the meeting, now you have a fine to pay as well.

No one ever benefits from rushing. It causes you to make mistakes, look unprofessional, and, in the end, adds more problems than solutions. So calm down, and don't rush during your phone interview. You have this time, so make the best use of it!

Pace yourself. Think of yourself as a long-distance runner, strategically exerting your energy where necessary in order to win the race. If you begin by immediately sprinting off the blocks, you will get exhausted halfway through and will not finish the race. You did not set an even pace and, therefore, you will end up losing to your opponent— the one who decided to run at a calm and steady speed. Conserve energy where necessary and drive to the finish line in a strong, consistent manner.

You are the runner and your phone interview is the race. There are many talented individuals competing with you to earn that top phone interview position—the one who gets to move on to the next step, the face-to-face interview. You need not rush to impress your interviewer. Instead, be the calm, evenly spaced runner who uses intelligence rather than speed to gain that top position.

SAY YOUR NAME

There is nothing more important than your name. When people say your name they think of you, your personality traits, and your accomplishments. Hearing your name makes you feel wanted and needed. It also is important in building relationships with other people.

You want your phone interviewer to know your name. You are not just another candidate. You are one-of-a-kind. Be sure your interviewer learns your name by using it throughout your phone interview. You can strategically do this by creating scenarios that showcase your abilities using your name. For example, "Bill walked into my office and said, '[Your Name], what do you think we should do about the situation with the finance department?'" This way, you give an example of a smart decision you made at your past employment while linking your name to this achievement.

This example of self-awareness shows the interviewer you know who you are and are comfortable and confident with your own skills. These are key assets to display during your phone interview.

Saying your name also reminds the interviewer of your name. Think of it as branding. When something has a particular brand name, it is memorable. It's not just a soda, it's a Coca-Cola. It's not just a car, it's a Mercedes. Brand names carry meaning and certain attributes that are attached to them. Do the same for yourself during a phone interview. You are not just a candidate; you are Jane, the best person for this job. Be sure your interviewer knows your name in a comfortable, meaningful context.

Something to Think About...

Think of a time when you started something new— started a new job, attended a new school, or moved to a new neighborhood, for example. You met many people within a short amount of time. The people with whom you are going to start up a conversation after that initial meeting are the ones whose names you remember. This is because something clicked when you met them that made you interested in continuing to build these friendships. Thus, the personality traits connected to their names stuck out in your mind.

You can use this same technique on your phone interview. Say your name, using it in positive, professional situations. Your interviewer will remember your name and the great attributes associated with it. This leads to a positive relationship between you and your interviewer that will help you ace that phone interview and continue to the next step.

Using your name sets you apart from the other candidates, making you a unique, valuable individual. Use your name on your phone interview in order to stand out in your interviewer's mind. Your name is your brand, so use it!

SAY THE PERSON'S NAME

There are three strategic places to use the interviewer's name: during the greeting, during the question and answer session, and at the closing of your phone interview. This is a sign of respect and acknowledgment of your interviewer as a professional human being. This will boost his ego and also boost your performance on your phone interview.

You need to say the interviewer's name at the beginning, middle, and most importantly the conclusion of your phone interview. Begin with "Hello, Mr. Jones," "Hello, Your Honor," and so on. Be sure to use the correct greeting based on the level of the position and the cultural factors of a phone greeting in this particular scenario.

Do not overuse your interviewer's name. This would demonstrate you are consciously using his name, implying that you are nervous and acting unnaturally. Use your interviewer's name in a genuine, respectful manner throughout your phone interview.

STORY WITH A MORAL

I once was conducting a phone interview and the person I was interviewing continually said my name at the beginning of every statement. Not only was he overusing my name, he often confused Paul with

Peter. This was not only distracting, but also incredibly annoying. It reminded me of little kids who have just learned to talk. At first, parents are very excited to hear their child say Mommy or Daddy. However, by the end of a day full of toddlers screaming "Mommy!" or "Daddy!" parents often do not want to hear their names anymore.

Moral of the Story: Use your interviewer's correct name three times throughout your interview. This is positive and professional without being overdone. Use, but don't abuse, your interviewer's name.

USE VIVID WORDS

Use vivid words during your phone interview to create an image in your interviewer's mind. Which sounds better?

- ✒ I saw a bird out my window.
- ✒ I gazed out my window and observed a bright yellow hummingbird among the flowers.

In this same descriptive manner, vivid language will create mental images of who you are, your abilities, and what you can do for the organization.

- ✒ "I am a financial engineer," rather than, "I am in finance."

- ✒ "I am a leader who motivates and influences my team members," rather than, "I am a manager."

℮ "I am a highly qualified individual who can cut costs and increase revenue for your organization," rather than, "I would like to work for your organization."

Use beautifully crafted and passionate words to create a mental video in your interviewer's mind. Make this person want to hire you. The correct insertion of vivid words during your phone interview will guarantee you will be remembered by the interviewer.

Something to Think About...

Think of a poem or short story that you particularly enjoyed reading. The descriptive adjectives that create attractive images in your mind make this more entertaining than a textbook or instruction manual. As you read the vivid words, you became a part of the poem or story, not merely a reader trying to get to the next stanza or chapter.

When something sounds pleasant and can be imagined, it is much more interesting than memorizing dates and procedures. This is what you want to do on your phone interview. Be the poet who draws the reader in with words that are enticing and vibrant. In the same way, draw your interviewer in by using vivid language that makes the conversation interesting.

Descriptive words are important and necessary on your phone interview. They allow your interviewer to envision you and your abilities bringing success to the company. This will make you stand out from other candidates and help you ace that phone interview.

GET TO THE POINT

There's no need to dance around the topic at hand; this is an interview, and you both know why you are here. Get to the point by speaking in few words—in sound bites.

If someone asks, "How was your day?" you wouldn't respond with a play-by-play of everything you did that day from breakfast until you went to bed. Instead, you'd respond with "good," "fine," or "great," depending on how your day went. Short, simple, and to the point.

Don't waste your valuable phone interview time with meaningless words. If you have the "gift of the gab," try to put that gift aside during your phone interview. Fillers are unprofessional and unimportant in this context.

Think of the last page of any chapter in a textbook: the summary page. This last chapter pulls everything together to make key points in the chapter. Your phone interview is similar to having multiple summary chapters. You want all the high points and all the sounds bites pulled together so it creates an impressive story. You want to get to the point as quickly as you can. You look smarter, more professional, and you make a much better impression when you get to the point in a very simple manner. Be bold. Be brief. Be done!

STORY WITH A MORAL

I have a client who really goes into a lot of detail when answering a question during a phone interview. After a few minutes of listening to her, I am sure potential hiring managers are tuning her out. Someone who talks excessively is not getting her point across. Quite the contrary, she is aggravating her listener. This will not be beneficial to your phone interview.

Moral of the Story: Do not be my rambling friend during your phone interview. Say less, mean more, get to the next step!

Sound Bites

Keep your answers brief and to the point so that the interviewer:

- ☏ Will be able to remember and record what you say.
- ☏ Can recognize your main points.
- ☏ Doesn't become distracted by unnecessary words.

Succinct responses place you in a positive light because:

- ℂ Such responses will prevent you from rambling, making it seem that you're avoiding the question, or that you're misinformed.
- ℂ Direct answers imply confidence, whereas avoiding questions suggests insecurity.

Remember: This is a professional interview; it's not a phone conversation with an old high school classmate. Eliminating background stories and unnecessary information allows the interviewer to assess your strengths specific to the job opportunity.

Make your responses short and sweet. This will leave a lasting impression that will allow your interviewer to later reflect on your interview as a positive experience.

Something to Think About...

How do you learn to talk in sound bites? It's simple: Watch the daily news. I like to watch the news every morning while eating my breakfast to keep up with what is going on in the world. I am always impressed by the speaker's ability to quickly tell all that is "up next" right before a commercial cut. These promos right before the break are quick sound bites that keep you interested in the news. These few words create an image in the viewer's head that capture his or her imagination and curiosity, causing me to pour another bowl of cereal and settle in for the upcoming news stories.

News agencies are experts at creating sound bites. Watch and learn from them and you can be too! Use sound bites to capture the attention of your listener during your phone interview. Direct, concise sound bites are a powerful method of conveying knowledge in a professional and interesting manner to your interviewer.

SAY HOW YOU FEEL

The easiest way to let someone know how you feel is to say it. This completely eliminates any confusion in a conversation—especially a phone interview.

The interviewer wants to get a feel for you and how you feel about the position and company. He wants to know not only if you can do the job efficiently, but also if you would *want* to do the job and if you would be happy. No one likes a grumpy worker. Why make the interviewer play a guessing game about your attitude and emotions? This only takes away from the content of your interview. Rather, just say how you feel when the appropriate time comes. Use exciting, powerful words to translate how you feel. You have to really mean it in order for your voice to convey excitement. Let the interviewer feel the passion in your voice as you say, "*I want this job!*" Use feeling words at the right time and in the right dosage—don't overdo it! You only want to say positive feeling words, no negatives. You want to be very professional.

During your preparation, you may want to have these phrases posted at your desk so you can remember to say them during your phone interview:

- ✆ I am very excited about this position.
- ✆ I am very passionate about making organizations more efficient.
- ✆ I love being a senior leader.
- ✆ I am thrilled to be discussing this opportunity with you today.
- ✆ I am very interested in this position.
- ✆ I would be very happy to be part of your organization.

Use positive feeling words during your phone interview. Make it easy for the interviewer to remember your emotions during your interview.

Something to Think About...

Have you ever been in a relationship with someone and you cannot gauge how he or she feels about you? Maybe it is someone you have known for many years, but when you get together, you are unsure whether he or she is happy to be spending time with you. These types of uncertain relationships leave much to be desired.

You do not want to build confusing connections like this with your phone interviewer. It is not a guessing game. Do not make her guess if you are really interested in this position. Say how you feel. Spell it out that you are very excited about this opportunity. Clearly display your enthusiasm and your interviewer will feel the same. Be meaningful, be memorable, be powerful.

ASK KNOCKOUT QUESTIONS

Asking substantial questions shows off your intellectual curiosity. It proves you are actually interested in obtaining this position and want to learn everything there is to know about it. This reflects your dedication to responsibilities, placing you in good standings for hiring.

There are many negative consequences to remaining silent during your phone interview. Candidates who are not inquisitive give off the impression that they:

- ℂ Lack the intellectual ability to form questions.

- ℂ Lack the confidence to ask questions.

- ℂ Think they are too good to need to ask questions.

By contrast, candidates who ask multiple questions can:

- ℂ Prove they are paying attention during the phone interview.

- ℂ Prove they are interested in the position and the company.

© Prove they don't feel insecure about clarifying information.

Ask questions that will impress the interviewer and display your professional abilities. Your curiosity could even spark questions the interviewer has never considered; hence displaying your insights. Remember: The only dumb question is the one not asked.

Something to Think About...

Have you ever watched a presidential press conference? Do the reporters pushing their way to the front to ask, "What did you eat for breakfast today, Mr. President?" Certainly not. They ask five-mile-long questions that take multiple breaths to get the whole thing out! These are knockout questions. They contain economic, financial, and political components. These are the types of questions you want to ask during your phone interview.

A knockout question is not a linear question. "Mr. Jones, does your company produce watches?" Response: "Yes, we do." This question does not stimulate conversation or offer room for expansion of a discussion. This simple question and simple answer portray a simple thought process. This will not impress your interviewer. A more impressive question would be, "A number of financial analysts have recommended your company as a possible takeover target from your number-one competitor. What do you see are the reasons for such speculation, and what do you think the impact will be to your market segmentation if this does happen?"

Remember, the questions you ask are more important than the answers you give during your phone interview. A sign of intelligence is in the questions a person asks, not in what he talks about. Asking intelligent, knockout questions can be difficult, but remember—this is an open book test! Do your research and have your knockout questions written out on a paper in front of you during your phone interview. I guarantee the interviewer will never know you are reading from a piece of paper. I've tested it numerous times and not once did anyone indicate that they knew I was reading from a piece of paper.

Step into the shoes of a big-time reporter at a major press conference. Ask those knockout questions. The questions you ask during your phone interview will demonstrate your professional and intellectual ability—make them count!

SOLVING, NOT SELLING

"Buy! Buy! Buy!" screams the Wall Street broker. "Buy Now! Don't worry about the stock, just buy!" This is the speech of a seller. There is a huge difference between trying to sell yourself on a phone interview and proving you can solve a problem. You want to be a solver, not a seller.

Think about how you feel when someone is trying to sell you something and she is working really hard at it. Do you feel she has your best interests at heart, or is she just interested in making a sale and benefitting herself? A seller wants to close the deal and wants your money, not your problems.

If you try to sell your best attributes during a phone interview, you are not going to get the job. This is because a seller does not come across as someone who is there to better the corporation. A seller is someone who is interested in his own profit and is not someone the interviewer is inclined to trust.

Think about people whom you trust and confide in to help you along the way. These people will help you solve your problems, even if it means going a little bit out of their way. These individuals (the solvers not the sellers), are much more likely to be put in charge of that big corporate project.

During your phone interview, you want to be the solver. Tell the interviewer how the company will benefit from your employment. What key attributes will you add to make the team more successful? It is not about you, it is about them. Remember, you are not trying to sell yourself on a phone interview.

Something to Think About...

Let's compare these two scenarios in a furniture store. In Store A, the salesmen immediately swarm you at the door, they tell you their names, usher you to the most expensive sofa, and don't allow you to take a breath before they have their order forms out and are asking for your last name.

In Store B, a friendly salesman approaches you, asking if you need assistance. You tell him you need a sofa that will fit in a corner, but you are not looking to spend a fortune. The salesman shows you a variety of options, showing you which couches come in a shape to fit your room. After making your selection, the salesman realizes all the drivers have left for the day, so he offers his own car and assistance to move the furniture to your home on his way home. This man has gone out of his way to accommodate and solve your problems.

Which person are you more likely to consider your trusted furniture advisor? Certainly store B, where all your wants and needs were taken into account, as opposed to the wants and needs of the salesmen.

Do not be a seller during your phone interview. You want to be the trusted advisee, the person whom the hiring manager can trust to solve the company's problems. You must look for solutions, not sales deals, during your phone interview. Be a solver and your phone interviewer will be sold on you!

Make Money, Save Money

There are the only two reasons why organizations hire people—to make money or to save money.

During your phone interview, you need to elaborate on how you can help the company make money or save money. Everything you do and say should resonate around these two key themes. These are the main grounds for hiring an individual. Being liked comes into play after doing a great job. Doing a great job is measured by money-making or money-saving. Corporate organizations want to grow and prosper. They want to be in control in the business world. How does a company gain control? How do organizations expand to more cities with new, innovative products? It's simple: by making and saving money. Show that you have this ability and you will prove to be a valuable candidate for this position.

Story With a Moral

I once conducted a phone interview with a candidate who was perfect for the job. She was professional, articulate, and clearly had done her homework prior to her phone interview.

She was everything we wanted in a candidate for this senior-level position; however, all her examples and situations that she calmly and clearly explained never touched on making or saving money for her past companies. Unfortunately, even though she had the skills and the intelligence, she was not offered the position because she could not drive it home— she could not measure up in terms of making and saving money.

Moral of the Story: Don't let all your hard work surrounding your phone interview go to waste. Be sure to clearly present your ability to increase the potential and success of this organization by making and saving money.

WHAT NOT TO SAY ON YOUR PHONE INTERVIEW

Don't talk yourself out of a job. On your phone interview, you always want to stay positive and to the point. You don't want to cross the line on being negative or offensive.

Here are common phrases you *don't* want to say on your phone interview:

- ℭ "My last company was terrible." The interviewer might wonder, "Will this candidate say the same thing about our company?" This will also lead her to consider your work attitude. A pessimistic worker is not a successful worker. If you truly think your last company was terrible, keep it to yourself. Don't share this information on your phone interview.

✪ "My last boss was a jerk." Again, your interviewer, especially if she is a hiring manager,
will wonder, "Will this candidate say the same
thing about me?" No one wants to work with
someone who trash-talks. This also implies that
you don't excel at working with others. Don't
say or give any indication during your phone
interview that you disliked or disrespected your
previous employer.

Don't use negative words such as *hate*, *dislike*, *can't stand*,
or *idiot* on your phone interview. None of these words will
help you during your phone interview. A negative tone will
only bring your interview down. Stay positive and use
positive words only. Don't go to the dark side; don't go
negative.

Don't bring up taboo items during your phone interview handshake or any other part of the phone interview
conversation. You want to avoid topics that are controversial
and could potentially start a debate. These include, but are
not limited to:

✪ Religion.
✪ Politics.
✪ Personal (children, hobbies, and so on). Some
small talk is good for conversation, but stick
mainly to work.
✪ Sex.

© Drug-related issues.
© Imprisonment.
© Race.

Focus on the main purpose of this phone conversation—the position for which you are interviewing. Stay concentrated on key topics concerning your experience, education, and how you can add value to this organization.

Something to Think About...

Have you ever been part of a conversation that suddenly turns awkward? You are standing with a close friend and he says something to a person you just met that makes you want to walk away and pretend you are not associated? He may not realize he said something inappropriate, but you do and you feel embarrassed for him.

The phrase "to put one's foot in one's mouth" is far too common in our society. Avoid this error during your phone interview. The easiest way to eliminate awkward, tension-filled moments is to leave out controversial and/or negative topics. Keep the conversation positive and focused.

Do not talk yourself into a negative corner during your phone interview. You do not want to be offensive or argumentative. Stay positive and focused to maintain a friendly atmosphere on your phone interview. Avoid the awkward, and the negative!

Don't Be Desperate

People want things they cannot have—Ferraris, BMWs, and exclusive club memberships—because most people cannot have them. The more difficult it is for something to be obtained, the more people want it for themselves. The same applies to your phone interview. If you seem overly available for the position (you need it, you will do anything to have it), you are not going to be hired. You cannot be desperate or beg during your phone interview. You will get a job. You do not have to act like the puppy dog that follows his owner around until he gets a treat. This will not inspire the interviewer to hire you.

What will increase your hiring possibility is if you are calm and confident. You know you are good for this position and you are going to perform this interview at your best. If it does not work out, then on to the next one! Your time and skills are valuable, just like the Ferraris and the BMWs. It is important to have this mindset during your phone interview. This self-confidence will be portrayed through your voice and eloquent tone, painting a positive image in the mind of your interviewer.

Something to Think About...

Think of a time when you were babysitting young children. When children want something, they often begin to whine, asking, "puhleeease?" Would you give children like this a piece of candy after they have been tugging at your hand all day? No, you would be annoyed and eager to get a break from their begging.

The same applies to your phone interview. An interviewer does not want to hear a desperate voice on the other end of the phone. This implies that you are panicky and lacking in self-esteem. These are not positive hiring qualities.

Do not beg during your phone interview. You don't need to; it is unnecessary. Be confident and assertive in your phone interview. Be the valuable, driven individual they should be desperate to hire.

YOU ARE IN DEMAND

Your psychological outlook is very important during your phone interview. You must remember that you are in demand! You are a valuable, professional individual—this interviewer should want to hire you! There are multiple dimensions to the in-demand role.

First, you need to show your interviewer that you are in demand. You are a busy individual. She does not need to know if you are busy babysitting the neighbor's kids or walking the dog; all she needs to know is that you are managing many responsibilities. You are a driven, highly active individual.

This also demonstrates that you have multiple opportunities before you. If the interviewer feels other companies are seeking your employment, she will be more inclined to want to hire you. She sees you are considered a valuable addition to a team by other people, and she will believe so as well.

The in-demand psyche is also important for your own performance on your phone interview. If you believe you are in demand, that you are a valuable contribution to society, then your voice will portray this confidence. Be careful not to be overly confident, because no one likes a pompous employee. However, having the mental outlook that many companies want to hire you will help to encourage you to display your key attributes at their best.

How do you formulate the illusion that you are in demand? When a representative from the organization calls to schedule an interview, do not accept the first offer. If he says Monday, you say Tuesday. If he says 1 p.m., you say 2 p.m. You are a busy individual! Your schedule is packed with important meetings and international calls.

Remember to use the home-field advantage tactic discussed in Chapter 1. Schedule your phone interview for the best day of the week and time of day for you—when you are at peak performance level. This will require some maneuvering of times and dates with your interviewer. By not accepting the first offer, you are psychologically embedding in the interviewer's head that you are a busy individual who is highly qualified and in high demand.

Something to Think About…

Think of a time you may have hired someone to do some work on your home. Maybe you were having an addition built or repaving your driveway. You called many different companies, asking for prices and timelines.

Say you narrowed it down to two companies and were comparing schedules. Company A said they were very busy. They have three different clients in the next town and two in the next state. They can work on your project on Tuesday or Thursday afternoon. Company B tells you that you are their only client right now—they can come work any day at any time. Which company are you more likely to choose?

Of course you are going to select Company A. Why? You know they must do great work because they are in high demand. Several other clients have trusted them and believe they will do a great job. They are clearly driven and highly productive.

Your phone interview should mirror the story of the successful paving company. You are Company A and this project needs your skills, which you have already demonstrated must be of high quality because you are in such demand.

By giving off the impression that you are a busy person, you are proving to your interviewer that you are talented, highly valued, and responsible for multiple tasks at once. Leave the impression with your phone interviewer that you are always in demand. Be in demand and they will demand to have you!

7

THE FINAL STEPS TO SUCCESS

Closing your phone interview is just as important as how you begin your phone interview—with respect, kindness, professionalism, and a human connection. You want to be remembered and leave a positive last impression at the conclusion of your phone interview.

THANK YOU!

Remember to say *thank you* at the conclusion of your phone interview. These are two very powerful words that are too often forgotten. While preparing for your interview, make a Thank You sign and place it somewhere on your desk where you will be sure to see it as your interview is winding down.

Forgetting this phrase during your closing could be detrimental, as it is discourteous and very unprofessional. Instead, thank your interviewer with enthusiasm in order to:

- ✆ Demonstrate appreciation to the interviewer for taking time out of her day to get to know you.

- ✆ Display politeness, which is a quality that enhances the possibility of your being hired. No one wants a rude coworker.

- ✆ Show you truly care about receiving this job and therefore are grateful for this opportunity to have an interview.

- ✆ Leave a lasting impression of a pleasant and sincere individual.

As you can see, this simple phrase carries a lot of importance. It is the first step in your concluding timeline. These two words, said with sincerity, carry a lot of power.

Something to Think About...

If you helped your neighbor carry groceries into his house and he did not say thank you, would you be inclined to help him again next week? Of course not; in fact, you might even complain to a friend about the rude individual you encountered. On the other hand, if he did display gratitude, you would be more likely to assist him in the future, thus developing an appreciative relationship.

This also applies to phone interviewing. If you demonstrate gratitude, the interviewer is going to think of you as a considerate person and be much more inclined to recommend you for the position.

Say Thank You Three Times

I suggest you say *thank you* three times in relation to your interview:

1. At the conclusion of your phone interview, a spoken *thank you* is most appropriate. Before you hang up the phone be sure to say "Thank you for your time. I greatly appreciate your time and consideration."

2. Within 24 to 48 hours after your phone interview, send a thank-you e-mail. Remember to include the reinforcement of all the positive aspects of your phone interview. You want to remind the interviewer what a great candidate you are for this position.

3. Then send a handwritten thank-you note, the way people corresponded before computers. This is a personal way to relate to your interviewer.

Thank-You E-mail

The thank-you e-mail is a key component of your job campaign. The main focus of the e-mail is to enhance your relationship, to showcase your professionalism by expressing appreciation, and, most importantly, to strengthen your position as the perfect candidate for the position. In the e-mail, you want to:

- ✆ Stress your strengths and qualifications.

- ✆ Provide additional information based on your phone interview conversation.

- ✆ Reaffirm what makes you special above all other candidates.

- ✆ Focus on two key areas: low you can make the company money, and how you can save the company money.

- ✆ Express your sincere appreciation.

Sample E-mail

Dear Mr./Mrs._____:

I want to thank you for your time and consideration for interviewing me on Monday, June 1st for the manager of technology position. I enjoyed our discussion, and the information you shared with me concerning ABC Company was exceptional. I am excited about the possibility of joining your organization.

I outlined key areas we discussed during our phone interview, aligning your needs and my capabilities that will allow me to make a significant financial contribution to the bottom line.

Leadership and Management Qualifications:

- "Roll-up your sleeves and get the job done" leader
- Highly effective in leading mid- to large-size organizations
- Created enterprise-wide executive leadership program

Results:

- ✓ Highly effective in driving team members to success
- ✓ Highest performing teams (based on survey results)

Planning Qualifications:

- Pioneered technology project management discipline
- Responsible for enterprise-wide technology resources

Results:

- ✓ 100 percent increase in IT product launches

Again, thank you for your time and consideration. I look forward to meeting you in person.

Sincerely,

Joe Smith

Thank-You Card

Remember, the proper way to thank a person during a professional encounter is through a thank-you card. This demonstrates that you put valuable time and energy into thanking your interviewer. It is sincere and meaningful. The detailed e-mail describing your value to the organization that you sent 24 hours after your phone interview is not enough; you need to send a handwritten thank-you card.

The card should not have cartoons on the cover, or glitter or confetti inside. It needs to be a professional thank-you card. The best thank-you cards are made from the highest quality paper with raised lettering. This type of thank-you card is very professional and business-oriented in its appearance and quality.

What do you write in your thank-you card? You are not selling anything in this card—you are thanking the person. Keep it short and simple. *Dear Ms. Jones, Thank you for your time and consideration. Sincerely, [Your Name].* That's it. Nothing more, nothing less. She may not even open your card, but she will know you sent it. This one act of human kindness will cause the interviewer to remember you in a positive light.

Story With a Moral

I was interviewing for an executive-level opportunity, and every person in the company whom I met received a thank-you card from me. Eventually, I was offered the position and accepted it. I noticed all the people with whom I had interviewed still had my thank-you cards in their offices, either on their desks or posted on their walls. I thought this was strange that they had kept this small note, so I asked, "Mary, why do you still have the thank-you card I sent during my interviewing phase hanging in your office?"

She responded by saying, "I have been at this company for 15 years and, over the course of that time, have interviewed many people, but no one has ever sent me such a nice thank-you card before. The quality and the workmanship made it just too nice to throw out."

Wow, I thought to myself. I had never imagined my small thank-you card would make such an impact. Sending a thank-you card had definitely been beneficial in the final stages of my phone interview.

Moral of the Story: Send a thank-you card after your phone interview to demonstrate a human kindness and sincerity about yourself. Surely, it can only increase your chances of advancing in the hiring process. Thank everyone with a thank-you card.

You may be thinking three thank-yous is overdoing it, but these thank-yous prove you really want this position. They demonstrate your determination while also implying you are a respectful individual. It also helps you stand out. Being humble and kind goes a long way in a competitive job market.

With each additional thank-you, these people have gained more of your respect and attention. Your desire to help them again has increased, as they have shown their genuine appreciation. These thoughts are exactly what you want to imprint in your interviewers' minds. Show them you are truly thankful at a level that goes above and beyond other candidates. Out-thank your competition to really impress your interviewer and ace that phone interview.

I WANT THE JOB

So many candidates participate in amazing interviews, but when they walk away, the interviewer is unsure as to whether that candidate really wanted the job and will shuffle that person into the middle of the pack of applications. At the conclusion of your phone interview, be sure to express your interest, plainly and simply:

- ✆ I want the job.
- ✆ I want this job.
- ✆ I want the (title) job.
- ✆ I want this position.

One would think that after finding the position, re-searching the company, setting up the phone interview, and preparing for this interview, it would be clear that you want the position. However, you must seal the deal by clearly stating, "I want this job!" It is also a good idea to add, "And I will be a perfect fit because..."

This puts you in a position of power and also gives you the opportunity to speak intelligently about the company because, after completing the phone interview, you know exactly what they want. This impressive closer will prove to the interviewer that you are determined and driven.

Make sure you state this at the *conclusion* of your phone interview, not at the beginning. Opening with "I want this job" makes you sound needy, and it also will make it seem as though you don't have all the facts to make an intelligent statement regarding the position. Wait until the end of your interview to reinforce your keen interest in the position.

You want to end your phone interview on a high note by speaking boldly, clearly, and with confidence. Don't cause any confusion by trying to seal the deal with a potentially desperate "I want the job!" Instead, show how much you want the job by impressing the interviewer during the phone interview.

STORY WITH A MORAL

I was once conducting a phone interview with a candidate for a management position. The interview went well, but nothing too spectacular. There was nothing that made this individual stand out from the competition. Then, at the conclusion of the interview, this candidate earned those extra points that placed him above the rest. He said, "I am very interested in the work this company is doing. I believe I am a great match for this position, based on my background experience, which I have just shared with you. Mr. Bailo, I want this job."

This statement, as part of his closing remarks, proved to me this candidate's genuine enthusiasm regarding this position. His professional drive was evident through the confidence in his voice. This changed his phone interview from standard to great.

Moral of the Story: Be sure to include a clear statement about your desire for this position at the conclusion of your phone interview. Your tone is very important. Do not say, "I want the job" in a pleading voice. Rather, make this a bold statement that exudes professionalism and confidence. You've done all the work, now express your goal!

What if I Don't Want the Job?

You've done all your research, you've sent in your application, you've set up your phone interview, and now, as your interview is coming down the home stretch, you start to think that you don't want this job. The feelings you have developed toward the job throughout the phone interview are just not what you are looking for. I would still say "I want the job," because you still do not have the full story. Although you have accumulated tons of important information, you have not been to the site and actually met the employees.

Also, even if you are positive you do not want this job, you can still expand your networking through job search and interviews. You never know who you may meet at the face-to-face interview or where this could lead you.

Only when you have a written offer can you be sure you have all the information regarding the position. Then you can make the serious decision of whether you actually want this position. Until this point, continue saying, "I want the job."

STORY WITH A MORAL

I have a friend who was nominated to attend a weekend leadership seminar. It was a far drive and, from reading the brochure, she had determined she did not want to participate. Instead, she gave the offer to her sister, who agreed to go in her place.

Well, her sister came back on Sunday evening raving about the great skills she had learned and the new networking connections she had made. Although the pamphlet had made the conference sound as if the entire day was booked from start to finish, she explained that they had plenty of free time in the middle of the day to explore the surrounding city. My friend was very upset that she had turned down this opportunity. She had not had all the information clearly laid out before making a decision, and thus suffered the consequence.

Do not let this happen to you on your phone interview. If you are not feeling confident in the position or company, maybe it is just the angle from which you are viewing it. A conversation with a different person or a look at some additional responsibilities may completely change your attitude toward this opportunity.

Moral of the Story: Do not close the book on a job opportunity based on a phone interview. Continuing to express enthusiasm for this position will continue to open new doors in your career search. You always want the job, until you are absolutely positive that you don't.

The Follow-Up Timeline

At the conclusion of your phone interview, you want to begin your follow-up timeline. This consists of five parts:

1. Conclusion of actual interview: When you are still speaking with your interviewer you need to remember to say *thank you*. This will end your conversation on a positive, respectful note.

2. 24 to 48 hours later: Send an e-mail to your interviewer, summarizing what you spoke about during the phone interview. In the subject line of this e-mail, place your name and the position for which you were interviewing.

3. 24 to 48 hours after sending your e-mail: Send your interviewer the handwritten thank-you card expressing sincere gratitude for having taken the time to speak with you.

4. 24 to 48 hours after sending your handwritten thank-you: Send your interviewer the interesting news article about the company that you already found during your preparation research. This demonstrates intelligence and interest in the company.

5. 24 to 48 hours after sending your news article: Call to ask about the status of your phone interview.

Completing these five steps 24 to 48 hours apart from one another allows you to stay on your interviewer's radar for five to 10 days. As your interviewer is conducting phone interviews with other candidates, he is constantly being reminded of your stellar phone interview performance.

This follow-up timeline also demonstrates your professional and business-oriented nature. It shows you are a sincere and intelligent individual. Following these five steps will significantly increase your hiring potential.

ANALYSIS OF YOUR PHONE INTERVIEW

Immediately after your phone interview is completed and you hang up the phone, think about what worked, what didn't, and what you would've done differently. Rate yourself and be honest! No one else is going to see this piece of paper. Rating yourself allows you to keep track of your phone interviewing performance. It also helps you think of ways you can improve. You are already on the road to improving your skills by reading this book!

Remember, the goal is to constantly improve your phone interviewing skills to obtain the face-to-face interview to get the position you deserve!

Rate yourself on a scale of 1 to 10 (1 being the lowest and 10 being the highest).

Write down on a piece of paper (there should be one right in front of you if you organized and prepared well for your interview) if you were successful in terms of:

- ℂ Were you on time?
- ℂ Were you prepared?
- ℂ Did you feel confident?
- ℂ Were you relaxed?
- ℂ Was your voice clear and solid?
- ℂ Were you bold, brief, and to the point?

Next, determine what worked best for you and continue to improve on your less-developed phone interviewing skills:

- ℂ What didn't work for you?
- ℂ Were you late for your phone interview?
- ℂ Were you unprepared?
- ℂ Did you feel stressed?
- ℂ Did you feel uncomfortable?
- ℂ Did you talk too much?
- ℂ Were your questions not on target?

Something to Think About...

After a sports game, the news reporters often interview the captains of the losing team. They ask, "What went wrong?" What was going through your head out there?" These players typically answer by pointing out what they did well, but then comment on those plays that hindered their ultimate victory. They are doing the same thing you should do after your phone interview. Analyze how the game/interview went and determine how you can improve for the next time.

If pro athletes can do this, you can, too. Working on your weaknesses will make you a better phone interviewee, so it is important to recognize what they are. If you know your strengths and weaknesses, you will be better prepared next time around. Only by constantly improving your skills can you ace that world-class phone interview! Recognize, revise, and improve for next time!

How Do You Rate?

Want to know how well you perform on a phone interview or if you will be recommended by the hiring manager? Want to know how you rate against your peers?

Phone Interview Pro (*www.phoneinterviewpro.com*) can help you prepare for and strengthen the skills you need to ace your phone interview.

Phone Interview EDU

Phone Interview EDU is a fun, interactive evaluation of your phone interview IQ. It covers all aspects of the phone interview, with animation and explanations of the correct answers.

The Evaluation

Conduct a live mock phone interview with an executive evaluator who will assess your phone interview skills with a 250-plus-point evaluation. You'll receive a detailed, personalized analysis of your performance, including what you did well and where you can improve.

The Seminar

Your college, university, company, or organization can receive invaluable, hands-on information from the leader in the industry. Seminars are lively and interactive, and are individually designed to fit your particular needs. Get all your questions answered on how you can ace your next phone interview.

Don't Dwell on the Past

If your phone interview goes poorly, when it is done, get over it. So you didn't represent yourself correctly. You made some mistakes, didn't say the right thing—learn from it. You cannot go back in time, but you can impact the future. Work out your mistakes for your next phone interview, but never try to fix the one you just completed.

Many people have asked me, "What should I do about the fact that I did not represent myself well on my phone interview? Should I call the person back and explain?" The answer is no. *Do not* call your interviewer back after your phone interview to try to explain some mistake you made. It will only make you look desperate and unprofessional, and won't increase your hiring potential. This will almost never change the interviewer's view of you.

The goal is to do your best when it counts, not after the fact. Do the best you can on your phone interview and be satisfied knowing you presented the best portrait of yourself.

STORY WITH A MORAL

I interviewed someone for an opportunity and, from my point of view, the interview went well; however, the candidate thought differently. Fifteen minutes after our hour-long phone interview, I received a call from the interviewee to elaborate on a point he had made in the past hour. I found this very odd and it actually made me question the positive potential of the interview. If this person doubted his performance, should I doubt it as well? This added interaction did not change my thoughts on how he or his experiences related to the company. It brought no additional value to the interview, so why do it?

Moral of the Story: Do not try to fix mistakes you may have made during your phone interview. Learn from them for next time, but never dwell on what has already happened. In reality, trying to change what is already done will only complicate the situation and will not change your interviewer's opinion to a more positive one. You can't change history no matter how hard you try.

You Will Get a Job!

Don't stress: You will get a job. The only thing we don't know is when, where, or how much money you will earn. Just by reading this book you are proving to be diligent, intelligent, and seeking to increase your knowledge and sharpen your phone-interviewing skills. It is only a matter of time. You must stay on course—do not lose faith in yourself or in the skills you have learned throughout this book. Constantly improve your phone interviewing skills—practice speaking professionally when you are on the phone with friends and family.

What I am teaching you in this book is not only for your phone interviewing, but for your entire job campaign. Use these skills when filling out applications and interviewing face-to-face. Remember, every time you pick up the phone, you have an opportunity to impress someone. Take what we have taught you in the phone interview handbook and apply it to every job-related phone call, from making the phone interview appointment to calling to accept the position.

STORY WITH A MORAL

Don't ever give up faith in your job campaign. You are an intelligent, valuable individual. You will get a job!

I received an e-mail from a client whom I met at a Phone Interview Pro presentation. She had gone six months, battling interview after interview, but never landed a job. Finally, she had a phone interview that went incredibly well and she aced it! The company called her in for a face-to-face interview and she got the job!

Moral of the Story: Some job campaigns are longer than others. You cannot give up hope! Continue working hard to improve your phone interviewing skills and you will get a job!

You've come so far—have faith that you will get the job! Remember, you are not alone in your job search. There are people willing to help you! As always, be bold, be brief, be done!

INDEX

About the Author

Paul Bailo MBA, MSW, PhD (candidate) is the founder and CEO of Phone Interview Pro—a service for job-seekers who want to perfect their telephone job interviewing skills. Mr. Bailo recognized that although resume, interview preparation, and target company research assistance are commonly offered by outplacement and career counseling organizations, the importance of the telephone interview is often overlooked. In response to this, Phone Interview Pro has created a 250+ point phone evaluation not seen in the career services industry...until now! This is not only a new company, but also a whole new industry; it's exciting for us, of course, but the real excitement generated by Phone Interview Pro will come from those who hone their skills using the service.

Today, more than ever, job candidates make initial contact with prospective employers via the telephone. While making a career transition, Mr. Bailo determined that many candidates would welcome an affordably priced phone coaching resource. And Phone Interview Pro is the outgrowth of his experience.

And Check Out These Other Books

Be Your Own Best Publicist
How to Use PR Techniques to Get Noticed, Hired,
& Rewarded at Work
Jessica Kleiman and Meryl Weinsaft Cooper

EAN 978-1-60163-148-0
$14.99

Hired!
How to use Sales Techniques to Sell
Yourself On Interviews
Elinor Stutz

EAN 978-1-60163-142-8
$14.99

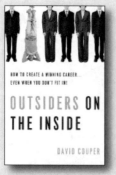

Outsiders on the Inside
How to Create a Winning Career...
Even When You Don't Fit In!s
David Couper

EAN 978-1-60163-127-5
$15.99

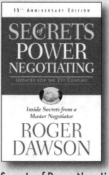

Secrets of Power Negotiating
15TH ANNIVERSARY EDITION
Inside Secrets From a Master Negotiator
Roger Dawson

EAN 978-1-601630-139-8
$16.99

To order, call **1-800-227-3371** or go to **CareerPress.com**

from **CAREER PRESS**

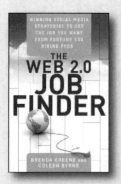

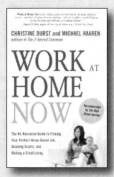
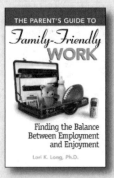